YESTERDAY TOMORROW

A letter to the Replacements

ANTHONY DIGIORGIO

ISBN: 1499209002
ISBN 13: 9781499209006

PREFACE

THE ONLY HONEST humans are young humans. We, their parents, adulterate their minds, adding morals and proper grown-up behavior in their syllabus of adulthood. In so doing, we turn them into confused liars. By the time these once-honest humans reach their mid-twenties, some begin to note the fallacies in their upbringing. Most of those who sense the deception in their parents' words and ways decide to pass that way of living on to their children anyway, and the drums beat on, driving the call to continued ignorance. The few that rebel, or keep questioning the ways of their parents, will eventually give up and start to conform because being an outsider has always been a hard way to live.

But there are rare cases, some who never give in to the constant drumming of religions, morals and ways of the parents. Those who choose to outcast themselves from society become wanderers in their own lands.

When I was young, my mother would call me *"fesso"*, "dummy," more often than she would call me *'ndo*, a variation of Antonio. Looking back, I see that she did it out of exasperation because I just did not fit into the brood that she and dad were raising. I was in my late twenties before I began to realize that I wasn't inferior to others, nor was I the dummy that she had inculcated in me. This revelation came when I figured out that I could walk and talk like most others, and that my real problem was that I had a thousand questions that seemed to have no answers.

Some people that I encountered along the way would spot my ignorance, tipped off by my questions, and act superior, as if I were truly the walking idiot that my mother had so often called me. Others were outright demeaning, while giving me insufficient and/or ill-thought-out answers. But there were a wondrous few who said, "Good question, and I don't know the answer." Eventually I realized that these were the most knowledgeable people.

In time, I read the books that some people talked about, read others that somehow interested me, and reached a point where I knew how to separate the possible from the probable. I even read a book on the great sayings of experts. To this day, I am still amazed that an English clergyman had the gall to say, "That God made man and woman with complementary sex organs doesn't mean that he wanted them to use those tools for coitus." Well, silly, if he did not intend them to be used for sex, why then has sexual intercourse been the only way to reproduce until a few short years ago? At times, it even produces idiots like him.

My education has led me here, where I am neither a deist nor an atheist. But I do think that if God was involved with the design of the human body, he was a poor engineer. No civil engineer would ever put the best amusement park ever discovered by humans in the middle of a sewage disposal system.

I even spent a couple of decades believing that Crito's apology to Sophocles, that injustice cannot be answered by injustice, was the best guideline to being an honorable patriot. Eventually, though, each new finding of truth and absoluteness was replaced with a seemingly better reality. I gave up on Diogenes – he never helped me find that honest man that I still hope exists. But in my years of seeking to learn, and to learn to think, no one would give simple answers to my simple questions. One of them was truly simple. The Bible says, "Thou Shalt not Kill." Yet we went to wars, we killed in self-defense, and we even killed murderers. So many people live with the belief that we should not kill, yet we do it anyway, and call it an honorable act. Why?

So I started thinking about things that interested me, with that same mind that my mother called "inferior." With time, I began to conclude that humans are a confused gathering of people traveling an endless, circling road. It is a road that offers the same repeating views, from generation to generation. There are no distance markers to let us know our location and the distance traveled. Worse, it is crowded with humans who are compelled to inform all other travelers on the road about the need to adopt the right religion, the right morals, and the right way to do things.

Now, my mind rife with senility, I can say that I have finally figured it all out. And it was simple. You are born ignorant, and you need a lifetime to understand that simple fact. The billions who follow the ways of their parents are the lucky ones, for they spend their lifetimes being purposeful. The irrational deviants at the edge of the masses of conformists, such as I, are the dummies. The best that we, the dummies, are going to do is learn that simple conclusion after we obtain answers to our thousand or so questions. But we also know that there are billions and billions more questions that need answering. My semi-literate mother was right after all. It took a lifetime to finally accept that I am an unlearned dummy.

I hope you find this interesting and that you understand my views. We, those who are about to die, are leaving you a world comprised of human travelers on the circular road to nowhere. I also will try my best to convince you to get off this road and start traveling your own road. Your own journey will have real landscapes and hills and meandering rivers, lots of anxiety and lots of hope, and the realization that in the end you are an educated dummy.

A. DiGiorgio

ACKNOWLEDGEMENTS

DURING MY LIFE I have met and lived through a few nice and many strange and even terrifying moments at the hands of other people. As I mulled the meaning of what happened in those moments I tried to believe that people just cannot be categorized neatly into good or bad people.

Deep down, that belief failed me, and eventually I began to live by a tenet that people can indeed be labeled. Good or bad, two categories. And it has worked out rather well for me.

September 1958, Long Island City High School, Home Room 314 was assembled in the auditorium. Mr. Dente was the teacher, and it was my first day of school in America. Mr. Dente asked me a question and I could not answer it because I did not understand the English words. Sitting next to me was a fellow student, who was taking Spanish, and he translated the words in Spanish, and I understood.

This fellow helped me through the next three years of school and eventually got me interested in Amateur Radio, which in turn led me to a career in electronic engineering. There is no way to repay a human being like Constantine Galitsis, my schoolmate Dino, who freely helped me so much. I hope he has had a good life.

February 1964, Academy of Aeronautics, Flushing, NY, I was listening to Mr. K., my counselor, speaking English heavily accentuated with German, calling me stupid, face to face. I had failed and was being kicked out school. I have always thought of him as an asshole. This, even though I knew that his formal schooling in Germany had been aimed at achieving Herr Hitler's goals: *"The weak must be chiseled away.*

I want young men and women who can suffer pain. A young German must be as swift as a greyhound, as tough as leather, and as hard as Krupp's steel."

Whereas I am immensely thankful to those that have helped me, I do have a higher obligation towards those many assholes who were never able to discover whatever little knowledge was mixed in with my ignorance, and proceeded to take the low road. They treated me like a leper.

Whereas the Good Samaritans helped me and then obligated me to pass on good deeds to others, the egotistical, know-it-all SOBs set up my boundaries. They showed me what not to be.

I can attest to the simple fact that whenever someone wanted help from me, I never acted like you, you the smug and self-satisfied who seemingly owned the world because of the little knowledge you had, that knowledge I did not yet possess. You made me strive to learn so that I would need your kind less and less.

You have provided me with miles and miles of yellow crime tape that marks off your world from mine. So, thanks to your being a self-righteous asshole, you have helped me be much different from what you are.

Again, Dino, Molte Grazie

Tony DiGiorgio

A LETTER TO THE REPLACEMENT

ON THE FIFTH of May, 1958, I arrived in America. I got off the ship at the 42nd Street pier on the west side of Manhattan. As we came off the gangplank, I spotted an uncle with the customs agents, and I saw him slip money to them after our luggage had been identified. Immediately, the agent put a chalk line on each piece. That is the way things were done in Italy, and America was no different. My second impression of America was how smelly and noisy the place was. I was a skinny and stupefied 15-year-old kid and was truly at a momentary loss when I did not see any cowboys riding down Fifth Avenue or on the Queensborough Bridge.

My third memorable impression occurred a few weeks later while riding in a car and seeing the lights on Steinway Street change sequentially. I don't remember ever seeing a traffic light in Italy, but here they had someone changing them in sequence. That was amazing to me. In less than three months, I fell in love with everything American. I consciously made up my mind to be an American. In time, I even became ashamed of having been born and raised in Italy.

Ten years later, I was working as a civilian tech rep in Vietnam. I could design the timing circuits for the traffic lights that I had seen on Steinway Street, if I had been asked to do it. Instead, I was teaching pilots how to use a new bombing computer to drop a bomb from 15,000 ft. at 480 KTS in a 60-degree dive and hit a target within 250 feet. In Vietnam, I began to question my love affair with America after seeing so many very un-American events occurring so frequently all around me. I unknowingly began to live in a tormented state (which, though much abated, exists to this day). I turned into a critic of the country that had given me everything I had.

Now, more than half a century later, old and fat and wanting only to be able to drink my daily dose of medicinal alcohol to tolerate my remaining days, I find myself wondering about my death. I would like very much to be of vivid mind, to be aware of death rather than waste away in a vegetative state. I did not sense birth, but I do want to sense death. I should be allowed to be aware of at least one of life's transition points. Since I am at the first stage of becoming a financial burden on society, I am hoping for death to occur soon. Of your monthly taxation, $1,100 goes toward my federal retiree health insurance. Another $2,200 comes to me from my federal pension, an unfunded benefit, and another $1,600 arrives from Social Security, another unfunded benefit. Since retiring, I have yet to thank you for having paid me about $5,000 per month, year in and year out. Thank you. You do understand that it would benefit all if I were to die and stop being a parasite?

While waiting to exit this world, I have been wondering about the replacements, those youths who are, unknowingly, preparing themselves to replace their parents. I often fantasize about answering their unasked questions, such as, "What was it like to…" and "What would you do differently?" I would answer that America or Earth is nothing more than a motel room, and you are nothing more than guests, replacing the others. We, the present occupants that replaced those now dead, are slowly checking out, and few of us are honest enough to admit that we abused and profaned the motel room, and that is why it is less habitable for you than it was when we entered it. But since no questions like that will ever be asked, I am going to answer them as if they had been asked by telling you what I think, what I saw, and what I think should be done differently.

We humans are rather dumb, and humanity has a basic design flaw. It takes a lifetime to understand life, and by the time you get there, you lack the means to effect changes. We never really look at our ways. Had we done so, the elders would never send the young to die in the wars they start. Our understanding of this complex world is limited by our morals. For example, all of the present efforts at controlling pollution are aimed at fixing this or that. In reality, we have pollution because we have too many guests in the motel room. And some of these guests have habits that further foul the room. People my age and older provide no resources to humanity, but we consume the most resources, and we should be gotten rid of so that we would decrease the world's population and decrease pollution.

The problems we leave for you were created by us, or inherited by those who came before. At any rate, we failed to solve them. We failed because we failed to face our ignorance. It is ignorance that keeps us from humanizing humanity. Ignorance in the hands of the people gives us poverty, killings, hate, robbery, rape, wars, religion, selfishness, greed, discrimination toward those who are not like us and, most importantly, disrespectful behavior toward that simple motel room that is our environment. It is ignorance that sustains the imbecility of those extreme Americans who want to change America to an Aryan nation or to a welfare state. Modern government is a constant experiment. But no matter the written limits and hopes of a government, the people running the government suffer human frailties: greed, avarice, ignorance, corruption, prejudice, xenophobia and a plateful of other flaws. And these frailties perpetuate the miseries of humanity. In America today, the experiment in governance concerns making the rich richer and abusing the poor even more. The following paragraphs contain just a few examples.

The Native Americans are an abandoned group of humans. First, their ways were destroyed by the newly-arrived Americans, who eventually re-located the original inhabitants to unfertile lands. Next, we claimed that they were a nation within our nation. Even our kind and nurturing efforts turn into different ways of killing these people. Read about the thrifty genotype and how the majority of Pima Indians suffer from Type 2 diabetes – their genes had adapted to store fat for lean times, but that trait resulted in obesity once they adopted an American diet. That's a neat way to do away with an entire race. Hey, Israel, look into the way we treat the Native Americans. It may facilitate your subjugating and diseasing more Palestinians and the others in the occupied territories.

Americans treat the Latinos like trash. Latinos, the resultant mixture of conquering Spaniards and Native Americans, had been "Christianized" and "civilized" 100 years before there was a Jamestown Settlement. The descendants of those people now come here to pick our vegetables, clean our commodes and do other menial jobs that Americans just do not want to do. All Americans, in one way or another, participate in getting that cheap labor from illegals and then treat them like servants. Similar to the John who uses a prostitute, it is OK to rent her and use her, but God forbid we acknowledge her as a human when we see her during her nonworking hours. And the sad thing is that the ancestors of every American, except for the natives, came here as an immigrant, just like the Latinos are coming to the 48 states above their borders today. This duality can exist only because of our ignorance.

It is ignorance that mothers dumb politicians in states where colleges excel in football but fail in education and where people want to force all Americans to do things as they do them back home. They are true examples of meager-minded and unwanted hooligans, who repeatedly enact the adage of bringing ham sandwiches to the royal buffet.

It is ignorance that fertilizes the minds of so many to believe that because their progenitors seceded from the Union, they have a right to brag about the idiotic act of secession, which killed so many and defended nothing but societal ways that in the end were as selfish as those found in the France of Louis XVI. Today, some of the children of those bigoted bastards brag about their forefathers' stupid acts while helping themselves at the tables of reconciliation, as if only good emanates from their impure hearts.

It is ignorance that lets idiots claim that abortion is a horrible termination of life but sending 18-year-old ex-hamburger flippers to die in undeclared wars is OK.

It is ignorance that created a judicial system with high rates of incarcerating innocents. More than two million Americans are in prisons. And how many innocent people have been executed by our incompetent legal system?

It is ignorance that has turned American Christianity into a money-maker for orators who sell what they don't have to poor, searching souls who have so little to give. Religion has fueled the fires of hate throughout history. Sadly, learned men and women subjugate themselves to it as if it were the answer to the unknowable.

It is ignorance that created an immense group of poor people and then bleeds away their last dollars with lottery tickets. Those poor souls, like religious fools, buy new tickets when their dreams die with numbers that were never chosen.

But ignorance is not what the other fellow is suffering from. It is what you and I are suffering from, and we don't even know it. Here are a few simple examples:

A pound of gold weighs less than a pound of potatoes, yet an ounce of gold weighs more than an ounce of potatoes.

The French, those people so detested by the American rednecks, wrote their constitution ten years or so after the US Constitution was written. Their document forbade slavery from the onset. In 200 plus years of trying, we have yet to achieve *egalité pour tout les americains,* as the French did so long ago.

There are supposedly seven billion humans on this earth. Of those, perhaps 100 million people in the medical and scientific professions know that it is osmotic pressure that keeps the blood of a pregnant mother from coming into contact with the blood of the fetus within that mother. The other 6,900,000,000 humans go on happily in ignorance of that fact, even though they all experienced it.

In the last century, there were three Americans – John Bardeen, William Shockley and Walter Brattain—who changed the way of life for all humans in a very good way. Maybe 100 million earthlings know about them, yet without their discovery, the lives of all seven billion people who occupy motel Earth would be much different. You don't have the slightest idea who these people were or what they did, but you use their creation daily. Here is more data about these three now-dead humans: none of them went to football powerhouse schools, none were reared in what we now know as the red states and one of them was a racist until his death.

Almost any American over 10 years old has heard about Elvis Presley. He gave us songs and rather poor movies, made a lot of money and died of a drug overdose. If you know about Elvis, but you can't fathom what I am saying about osmotic pressure or the three people above who changed the world, or you expect a pound of gold to weigh 473 grams, then you are among the majority, one of the ignorant humans. Go along for the ride, like most of your progenitors. Question nothing, and die more ignorant than you were born. How else can you describe humans who were born with a quest for knowledge, learned much in the beginning, and then walked the plateaus of ignorance for the remainders of our lives? Now we show our ignorance by proclaiming that the atmosphere is just as healthy as it was 1,000 years ago and that we did not create the pollution we deny. Or by accepting what 4 million members of the NRA say is good for all of us, even though that concept kills so many Americans each year.

Before we can fully understand our own ignorance, we must first question the belief Americans have that we are the best. We know there are countries where young girls are bartered in marriage even before they reach puberty or have their genitalia mutilated so that they do not get pleasure out of sex. In those same places, people still wipe their ass with their fingers. Because we are much better off than people in such places, we revert to the old cliché, "Yeah, we've got problems, but we are still the best country in the world." Comparing America to Third World nations is like comparing a college graduate from a famous football college to a graduate from a famous academic institution. For those who miss the logic, compare America to what America was supposed to be according to the Constitution; never compare it to countries where the best thing that can happen is for a fatherly dictator to control his people as if they were subhuman.

As you read this, try to understand that America does offer the best to all people when it comes to education. This book is about the majority of Americans who have lived in America for their entire lives with access to a superior educational system and opted to remain truly ignorant. Imagine being accidentally locked in a grocery store that closes for the weekend, without knowing how to escape or call for help. You become dehydrated and starve for the entire period. On Monday morning, when the store is opened, you come out crying that you are thirsty and hungry. This is what has happened—and is still happening—in a nation that has public libraries and public education; in such places as Pascagoula, MS (you must visit if you want to see how to enjoy stupidity at its best).

We produce such idiots as Trent Lott, Sarah Palin, Danny Quayle, and the dummy from Texas who wanted to be president, the B-movie actor who never won an Oscar but won the presidency, and thousands of others who fail to realize that they are only smart because they live among people who are more ignorant than they are. Of course, some Democrats are just as bad, but they encircle themselves with people who defend them, no matter what they have to do and say. What about the case of getting a blow job and not calling it sex and getting away with it?

America has the means to educate all its inhabitants, but the masses, like the idiot who was locked in the grocery store, choose to remain ignorant. And because of that, everybody suffers. So don't pat yourself on the back because we are the best. We are the best at killing each other, at making money, at killing people in other countries and at boasting the most miles of paved roads, yet buying the most four-wheel drives in the world to cruise these smooth surfaces.

I started admiring America in college. I believed every word about the Constitution and really felt that de Tocqueville had written the most telling truths about the new, free citizens of the world. Now, I think differently. America was formed as a government for the landed gentry. It wasn't meant to acknowledge you and me, the commoners, as full-fledged citizens. "For the people" and "by the people" were accidental qualifiers that are still evolving as modifiers of that government, to become more responsive to its common people. Its announcement occurred four score and seven years after the covenant of America, and it was issued from the mind of a rare man who was self-educated. Though George is credited with being the father of the country, I

believe Abe is the real American Moses. Anyone else would have set-
tled for a divided America, and the Southern gentry would still be
dueling away their differences. Before Abe, a tradesman or otherwise
un-landed commoner could not vote and had few rights.

Today, all Americans are guaranteed more personal civil rights
than were ever dreamed of by the founding fathers.

Now, twenty-two scores and five years after the creation of America,
we have another attempt by the moneyed scum to revert to the government of the rich, by the rich, and for the rich. A bunch of vagabonds
have entered politics and impeded the seesaw of governance by tying one
end to the ground and asking for ransom before they let it wave freely,
as it was designed to do. The Tea Party, the hardline conservatives, and
the liberals who chastise others but benefit from laws that put money in
their pockets, are either rich people or poor misguided idiots in search
of their version of utopia. Those who enter government service may have
patriotic goals in the beginning, but by the end they are greedy, scummy
bastards who lie, obfuscate and spend their energy convincing us that all
their issuances are good for us, no matter how painful or illogical. Senator
Proxmire and a few others like him are excluded, of course. These horrible times in which the few—Herr Cruz and his neo-Nazis, for example—
want to change America, not by existing laws but by outright disregard
for the welfare of the people. They are affecting the masses only because
we are the laziest, dumbest, most ignorant gathering of useless citizens
that America has ever mothered. The common American of today cannot
really be compared to the Americans of 225 years ago. Today's common
American is nothing more than a tool to the moneyed Americans, and
the more ignorant the common American is, the more probable it is that
he or she is a religious conservative, the easiest American to manipulate.
With that said, let me give you some examples of things that, in my opinion, are wrong with America, in the hope that you see where you fit.

1. We Are Fakes

The American way is the best in the world until you pay attention
to it. Why is it that we show so much brutality and killing on TV but

sexual intercourse is not allowed? Think about it. The Bible tells you to go and screw but not to kill. At the hands of the puritans, Americans have reversed it. Showing movies with endless killings is OK, but showing two humans screwing is vulgar. In case you have not figured it out, you were designed to screw, which is why it is joyful. You were not designed to kill, which is why you don't feel good about killing.

2. Is it OK with Israel?

The last 70 or more years of official American diplomacy with the Middle Eastern countries has been to develop a policy, get it blessed by Israel, and then send it to Congress. The process should be to develop a policy that is fair and does not hamper freedom for anyone, and then enact it. If Israel does not like it, simply tell them, "Welcome to nationhood."

3. In Good Times I Choose by Race, Creed; In Bad Times...

Americans are, by far, the best discriminatory obfuscators in the world. Take the case of an American in need of emergency assistance. He or she will pay no attention to the sex or race or religion or sexual attitude of a firefighter, a police officer or an emergency room doctor. That is the way we think when our asses are in a jam. But let someone talk about electing a female president, a Jewish president, or, just imagine, a *Hispanic* president, and out of nowhere, multiple reasons why this is a bad idea suddenly appear.

4. Some of My Best Friends Are Blacks

Closet racists, be they liberals, simple-minded rednecks or the majority of the white enlisted people in the US military, have problems calling the current president Mr. Obama. They hide their hate by referring to him as "the guy in the White House." They believe that every person on welfare is black or a Latino immigrant. The white, trailer-trash people in so many places in America are not welfare recipients. Just ask these righteous Americans who know it all.

5. Hey Stupid, This Is a Free Gift

Listen to a TV ad that wants you to buy something, and sooner or later you will hear the words "free gift." The ad people assume that you are so dumb that you don't know that a gift is free.

6. Hey Stupid, I Want to be Richer, so Send Money

Listen to TV infomercials in which someone tries to sell you a book with a step-by-step procedure on how to get rich. The only way that can work is for you to be as dumb as they guessed and make them a bit richer by buying the book. Others are selling books on how to strike it rich in real estate or get money from the government. Run and get your copy; the sellers will take your cash and not even thank you.

7. Lose Weight by Mimicking

There are times when the more learned people share their knowledge by expressing the wisdom that the best diet in the world is the Mediterranean diet. You heard about it—just eat like the people on the coast of the Mediterranean Sea, and you will slim down. They forget to tell you that those people also walk their asses off each day getting from point A to B. Again, the stupid people have suckered you in.

8. Get Your Free Erection Now

Better yet, buy these over-the-counter-pills and you will get an erection on demand, shed fat without exercising or eating less, and have better memory. They make their money, and you are still as you were before, except that you wasted money on pills and exposed your body to chemicals that might have damaged it.

9. What You See Is Not what You Get

Buy a packaged piece of fresh meat (although this is really a lie because the meat has been frozen and defrosted a time or two by the time it arrives in the display cooler), and you will find out when you open it that the bottom side of the meat, the one against the opaque plastic holder, is mostly fat, gristle and bones. It's nothing like the side with the clear plastic that suckered you into buying it. And this is not considered lying to the consumer. If it were, they would have been taken to court, right?

10. Pay Me to Make You See an Ad

You pay for cable or satellite TV, and enjoy watching infomercials for a good portion of the day. Here you are, paying someone to show you commercials in your living room, and the TV people have even convinced the FCC to run these commercials without running that little line at the bottom that used to say that it is a paid advertisement.

11. Yes, Cable TV and the NSA Are Watching You

The cable carriers know what channels you are watching and when. Think about that. By tuning to a cable TV channel on a cable system – which charges you much more than the service is worth in a true free market – you are being used to collect marketing data by the same company. And no one tells you that.

12. Why Should Poorer People Have Insurance?

Obamacare. If you are against it, you are even more stupid than you think. I am a retired federal civil servant. The workers you meet, even the ones making minimum wage in fast-food places, help pay $1,100 per month for my insurance, while I pay $440 per month. Yet these taxpayers have not been allowed to have affordable insurance.

Once insurance was made available for them, a few American bastards shut down the government because they wanted poor people to send money to the government to pay for my insurance and the insurance of other retired government workers. After all, how important are these poor peons in a system that respects only the moneyed? In case that is too complex, think about the government being a castle of yore with you on the inside of the castle and the peons sending all their goods to you and me in the castle. Is it OK for them to send their goods to feed the fat asses in the government? Why should they have any benefits? They are the modern day peons. This is what conservative Americans think. I got mine. Screw you.

13. Hello, Sardines

In America, every mode of public transportation is subsidized by the cities, the states and the federal government, except one. When you ride the bus or subway or Amtrak, the taxpayer is paying for a good part of that trip. If you get on an airplane, however, it is you alone against the airlines. By flying, you create more business for the government to tax than a bus rider, but you are mistreated in comparison to others. A bus or train rider gets five to ten times more space when traveling for less than an hour, and you, the airline passengers, are packed like sardines and treated like encumbrances by the overworked and poorly paid flight attendants. The government wants you to know that this is good for you. By the way, as you enter the plane and start walking to the back where you and I belong, look carefully and you will see your congressman in the first-class section. You have to look hard, though. Most of the time, the fat pigs bury their heads in reading materials so that they do not have to make eye contact with peons like you and me.

14. Heroes by the Millions

We are being brainwashed into thinking of our soldiers as heroes. This is wrong. It is disrespectful to those who were soldiers when soldiering was horrible suffering that was endured for the entire length of the conflict instead of today's short-term deployments. It is also disrespectful to call these part-time warriors heroes when other Americans, such as police officers and firefighters, face more dangerous situations daily. But there is a deeper problem with forgetting the past and heaping glory on the undeserving that most Americans fail to see.

a. Since World War II, the last war that America won, Americans have killed at least 2 million indigents in places like Korea, Vietnam, Panama, Afghanistan, Iraq and dozens of other places. In the process, we have also buried 150,000 or so American soldiers. And though we have not won a single one of these conflicts, Americans are led to believe that we are the victors. The first war in Iraq was not really a victory, if you consider that it had to be stopped because it was just carnage, without the other side fighting. Iraqi soldiers were even surrendering to media people.

b. Losers in wars do not celebrate. The Japanese and Germans do not hold yearly celebrations of the great temporary victories that they achieved in World War II. In America, however, we celebrate our victories and our losses as if they were the same thing. Not only does Hollywood make more money on conflicts that were initiated by the military-industrial complex, but the populace is steered into venerating our soldiers as heroes.

c. Our warmongering has taken such deep roots that we even have large groups of sickos who reenact battles of past wars. They take their youngsters to see war reenactments. When these people take a let's-go-to-a-picnic attitude toward war, they obviously fail to understand the suffering of war and disrespect the victims. The first battle of Bull Run attracted spectators, but they learned not to do it again after the battle spilled over into their picnics and a stampede of retreating soldiers forced the civilians to run for their hides. I wonder how many Americans know that we almost went to war with Peru in 1865 over bat guano. Imagine these sick people reenacting our victory/defeat of the Guanary War.

d. Beginning with the Civil War and ending with the Vietnam War, American soldiers were mostly drafted into service. Because of the rebelliousness that ensued after some wars (the bonus march after WWI and the Vietnam vets' protests), the country elected to go to a volunteer army. Now, almost 40 years later, we have the highest-paid soldiers in the world and the most coddled soldiers in the world.

e. Things are changing so fast that future soldiers will have contracts guaranteeing fighting times and rest times and the types of food and entertainment they receive before combat. A cold can of C rations during the Vietnam War tasted much different than a present-day warm MRE. Just imagine how the rations tasted during World War II. Those combat soldiers slept on the ground most of the time, and when sent to the rear for their version of R and R, they slept in tents with a dozen other soldiers. Today, we build barracks with plumbing and electricity, lounges and cafeterias, gyms and anything else to accommodate fighting troops as if they were stationed on a base in America. Of course, we do not tell the people back home about the whorehouses that spring up near these facilities, as they have, I'm sure, since the first war that humankind waged.

f. Then, upon their return home from another war that we never won but stopped for lack of interest, these heroes – who spent thousands of hours watching Internet pornography to pass the time on systems sponsored by the taxpayers –are treated as heroes.

g. Of course, today's soldiers see and endure horrors, but those who preceded them in World War II saw the same horrors in each battle they fought, and they fought many more than the modern mercenaries.

h. In case you didn't know, the deaths of the poor hamburger flippers who found better employment in the army enriched their survivors by $400,000 in untaxed survivor benefits. I'd bet you anything that if these poor, dead soldiers of our irrational xenophobic diplomacy had been given a truly free choice of what to put on their tombstones, some would have opted for something like, "Why did you kill me, you bastards?" But real freedom of speech is not granted even to those whom we send to die.

Our lack of participation in government and our lack of giving a shit about it all have turned America into a new Rome. We do not have an army of the people anymore. We have overpaid legions, netted from the lower echelons of Americans, who went from fast-food service to a grave or a life of disfigurement. Because of this, we can send people to die in aimless wars because the president and his lackeys decide it is in our best interest to do so. There are no more declarations of war or civil opposition to war, especially from the soldiers. There is no need to rebel, since those who died were young, ignorant souls born within a system of greed that cannot equally distribute education. If you live in a ghetto or barrio, you are not as good an American as the rest of us are.

Many of the mothers and mates of these poor dead bastards take the money and blow it and then hang the flag that lay on the victim's coffin in their trailers to hide the discolored paint. This is the most realistic view of our present American Hero, who was badly schooled and not given all of the opportunities that the sons and daughters of the moneyed people were afforded. You poor bastards. Now you are dead and out of the loop and are only insulted by our calling you heroes. Once every year, our benevolent, reminiscing hearts put a plastic flag on your grave, and the chances are that the flag is made in China.

15. I Am a Hero, Are You?

In World War II, the Germans had one fighter pilot who shot down 352 planes. The Americans also had aces, but if you took the number of planes shot down by the top ten American aces, it would be lower than that of that single German ace. With that said, the top American ace of World War II was a fellow called Richard Bong. He was pulled out of combat after his fortieth kill. He died on August 6, 1945, in Burbank, California, when the P-80, a jet fighter he was testing, crashed at take-off. This fellow is barely mentioned in American history. But as in all things American, there was a quite colorful fellow who shot down five German planes, broke the speed of sound, was rejected by the astronaut program and lived a long life who made millions from his fame. This proves my theory that before going to war, every soldier should be told that his major goal in war is to survive. The other stuff, acts of courage and superhuman feats, come only after the war and the only tellers of the stories are the survivors. Therefore, fuck the other stuff; it is all bullshit.

16. A Camp Follower is A Camp Follower

During the American Civil War, women followed the soldiers from place to place and tended to them, washing their clothing, cooking food and caring for the wounded. If you listen to NPR or History Channel features on these women, they are portrayed as nothing but pure angels. Of course, in my world of reality, some of them also provided other services, which though treated as a lower form of debauchery and depravity, probably took away the virginity of some soldiers before they died. A little sex will do away with fear, at least for a fifteen-minute coital quickie. Bless those women, but why not tell reality to those who follow us?

17. Government Whistleblowers

The US government whistleblowing program is the most un-American program that could have ever been generated. Here is why:

a. In America, your supervisors want to hear good things about their leadership, their programs and their chain of command. Stepping out of the loop and making them explain their errors to an inspector general is not tolerated.

b. In America, if you are so stupid as to think that an employer will not be sensitive to criticism, then you are the dumbest employee there. I was that employee.

c. In America, even the dumbest employee knows that when something is wrong, he or she will make a simple decision based on the answer to a simple question: "How much do I need this job?" The answer to that question should determine whether to report wrongdoing.

d. Providing inspectors general for government agencies and assuming these people will do what is good for the government, versus what is good for them, is truly a childish thought. An inspector general works for the agency that he or she is supposedly keeping in line. The top dog within that agency will decide the inspector general's promotions and pay raises. Therefore, believing that an inspector general is honorable and righteous is similar to believing that Mary was truly a virgin when she gave birth to Jesus.

e. Telling employees that they are protected when reporting problems is an outright lie. Imagine working for a husband and wife and reporting a fraudulent process to the wife in return for immunity. Dream on. Those two sleep together and not only share their bodies but share their minds as well. Of course, government managers don't share their bodies, but on a golf course many things are said.

18. Cheating on Travel Reports

Early in my employment with the US Navy, there was no requirement to provide hotel receipts when traveling overseas for the government. We were simply paid the full amount allowed for lodging. Some people would charge for the hotel stay even though they had gone to sea for a few days for work purposes. I did other things that were dishonest, but I was never as bad as that. We are all crooks, in small and big ways, but our individual crimes are never as bad as the crimes of the real crooks. Right?

19. How Much Overtime Do You Want?

I have worked for 15 or so employers during 56 years of living in America. Only the US Navy allowed me to charge unsupervised overtime. To this day, if you work for my former employer, you charge whatever overtime you feel you can get away with. Think about that. You get assigned a job on a ship and you work a few hours of OT, and then you turn in whatever totals you want, and all is OK. No one questions what you did during that time or asks for validation that you were even on the ship.

20. The Navy Hotline: Boss, We Got another Sucker Here

I was never a team player but once, long ago, I believed there were honest humans in the circles I frequented. When I worked for Litton, my first employer and a company that in the early '60s was a darling of Wall Street, there were cases in which I was told to tell marginal truths about equipment issues, and this really irked me. Once I entered civil service, I knew that I could report any wrongdoing. There was no way I could have ever imagined the abuses that exist within the government, both by the military and civil service people.

I started reporting what I felt were wrongdoings. I reported wrongdoings to the Navy hotline, senators, inspectors general and even to admirals in charge of programs that were wasting money or were grossly mismanaged. I did so much of it that one day, a higher-up told me, "Tony, give up on it. They have special trash cans marked with your name for all the things you write." Since I was never accused of being bright, I continued, and here are some of my observations:

a. I turned in my command for having three GS15s when they were allowed only one (GS15 is the highest rank you can make before going into the Senior Executive System ranks). One of these fellows was working on his PhD while employed by us, and his dissertation was on Total Quality Management. My employers justified his position to a senator by saying that he left the dissertation with them when he retired from government work.

b. I reported multiple incidents to our GS15, a human of a lesser integrity than those found in any penal system, and this SOB had someone investigate my accusations. The investigator talked to me and filed a report. Of course, the results were as the GS15 had wanted them. About 13 years later, just prior to his retiring, that investigator, a locally-grown, ex–shipyard favorite son (and, of course, a Christian SOB), came to me and explained that he had done wrong and asked me to forgive him. Being mostly a crude self-made man, I told him to fuck off.

c. The Navy has a local top commander that runs all of the activities in the Norfolk area. This office used to have a hotline. The number was posted in various places, and it assured that you could remain anonymous. The monitor and I had face-to-face dealings. She called me one day and, to the best of my memory, said, "Tony, we received an anonymous report on some problems, and the writing is so much like yours that I was wondering whether you had sent it in." This stupid human not only did not understand that she was legally prevented from identifying the submitter of such reports but was overtly trying to find the source by asking other people who had used the so-called protected process.

d. A first-line supervisor that I knew well, and who tried very hard not to be like the rest of the management gang, told me one day that they took two first-line supervisors and made them listen to an anonymous recording, trying to identify the speaker. Again, the recording was obtained from a hotline, advertised as confidential.

e. In the mid-'90s, I happened to walk by an open conference room and saw a lawyer, whom I had once employed, giving a seminar to first-line supervisors on how to survive whistleblowers.

f. My final whistleblowing at the Navy occurred in early 2003. My supervisor, the personification of a true American bigoted redneck, was a locally-grown leader of men. He went into the Navy, which taught him all he knew, and he got out after a few years. He got a job with us and was promoted to supervision. This fellow subcontracted a good-looking clerk from a local company that was run by a buddy of his. Then he dictated to us that we would report to this clerk for job assignments. I rebelled. By then, I had been paid as an engineer for over 30 years. I had reported to military officers, civilian engineers and even stooped down to civilian technicians promoted to managers, but I would be damned if I was going to take my orders from a clerk.

I wrote up the incident and other issues, such as the overt display of friendship, well beyond supervisor and employee, between the two. They would lunch together in his office, and if you walked in on them, you felt that you were dealing with a husband and wife. I made the mistake of reporting that when the idiots and thugs were in charge of America. Remember President Dicky and the idiot prince who had no brains, but no one who would tell him that? Anyway, the rednecks in my outfit, always a majority who reluctantly obeyed the rules of civil service, only when self-serving, had a free hand at imposing their ways.

I was given a punishment of five unpaid days for telling it like I saw it. I went home on sick leave, and a month later I qualified for early retirement. They gave me a $25,000 enticement plus a pension. I got a job with a company that refurbishes former US Navy ships that are sold to foreign countries, and I've been happy ever since.

I am a vengeful individual, and happy with it, and am still working out how to pay back my former supervisor. He has made things a bit difficult, since the SOB decided to die before I could avenge myself. But I still have time, and a mind, so there is hope.

The Navy whistleblower program was designed for honorable humans. If you are in charge of people and you make decisions contrary to the rules given to you, you are not honorable. Any institution in America, including the Roman Catholic Church, will claim to be honorable, but if you get to know the people in those institutions, you find out that honor either never existed there or died in its infancy. In a situation like this, a simple-minded employee like I once was always loses.

Furthermore, though managers seem incompetent, they are fully cognizant of the wrongdoing that goes on. For an employee to raise enough gumption to go to a third party and say that his or her boss is a crook is almost as stupid as an employee can get. If you are dumb enough to become a whistleblower, as I was for so many years, here are the probable results:

a. Your boss will call you a liar behind your back.

b. The boss will be protected by his or her superiors. It has to be that way, else the entire group falls. That is not going to happen. Look at the fat cats at the Veterans Administration. Of their 470 top managers, each received good reviews. This happened while the veterans seeking medical help died waiting. These are rough bastards who will protect their turf at all costs.

c. It will make your life miserable. The first thing they usually do is to call you a recalcitrant, a malcontent or a disgruntled employee.

d. You will not be sent to meetings anymore or allowed to participate as much.

Being a whistleblower is an honorable thing, but being a whistleblower while trying to feed your family is stupidity. Oh, and one more thing about being a whistleblower in a military system. Don't do it. You are fighting people who are trained to stick together and fight. If you do fight them, please make sure you read about a whistleblower of half a century ago who was fired by Nixon. This fellow was kind enough to help me with some of my problems. Mr. A. Ernest (Ernie) Fitzgerald was his name. He is the only successful whistleblower I know about. Right after you read about Mr. Fitzgerald, get a copy of Don Quixote and study it, because being a whistleblower will make you a hero in your own mind and nothing else.

21. I Am an Expert on 40-Year-Old Navy Equipment

The Navy buys equipment that it cannot maintain, so cadres of civilians are hired to help. In 1978, I started working for the Navy as a contractor at a place called NAVSEACENLANT. I was the 38th person to work in that office. We had 500 or so ships and fewer civil servants. Today, I still work for the Navy as a contractor on equipment that was designed and built in the early `70s. I have actually had the pleasure to work with a sailor and 30 years later work with his son on similar equipment. Today, we have fewer than 300 ships and at least 1,000 civil servants and contractors. And let's not forget that the navy spends millions on its own uniformed people to maintain the same equipment.

a. What used to be NAVSEACENLANT is now NSSA, but in a few months it might change. We used to be mostly engineers and techs that went to ships with no tools, no cheat data and no test equipment. Today, the reps go to ships with all of these. Thus, the Navy created a situation in which they pay for shipboard sailors to maintain the equipment, but untold numbers of civilians also make a living maintaining the same equipment. There's no way an American business would do that, but the Navy does it every day.

b. My old employer was composed of at least 95 percent civilian technical personnel, including a few handpicked enlisted people who wanted to learn more about the systems. Now, the place is at least half military. The people assigned to us are too busy fulfilling their Navy obligations to be full participants in our troubleshooting. The place has also become a dumping ground for limited duty personnel. At times fathers and mothers bring their children in because of problems with babysitters. There are many social and professional gatherings that these military people have to attend. There is even a lounge for those famous CPOs, aka NCOs in other services, but no lounge for engineers, or technicians, or supervisors, or even uniformed naval officers.

So, is the group of former engineers and technicians still a technical outfit? On paper, yes, but in reality it has become a uniformed shore command manned by civilians. Logic says that the original decision to hire technical civilian personnel on a permanent basis was necessary because of the uniformed staff's inability to fix all of their problems. Now, three to four decades later, the Navy has managed to mess up another working and useful process.

22. Did We Win That One, Too?

The US Navy and America seem to have the wrong concept for naming ships and holidays. The USS *Anzio*, USS *Bataan*, USS *Chosin*, and USS *Hue City* are all named after places where we either lost battles or did nothing heroic. The Alamo and Pearl Harbor were events where we got whooped, but they are also glorified. Why do we do that?

23. Highest Paid Janitors in America

My old employer, NAVSEACENTLANT, had a handful of janitors who collected the trash and vacuumed. Today, with Navy management at its best, we have higher-level staff doing trash, and somewhere some group of Navy managers can actually demonstrate that money is being saved. Of course, no one is counting the simple fact that each Navy petty officer first class costs at least $100K to $150K per annum. The civilian GS9s and above are just as expensive. So, does the Navy save taxpayers money? Just ask them.

24. No Poo-Poo but Lots of Gore

Why is it that in American cowboy movies you never see horses take a dump, yet we are entertained by human thespians puking? I have done my share of embracing the commode after excessive drinking, and to this day I do not believe there is any artistic value to it.

25. Paying for it Two or Three Times

Working for the Navy is most likely what it used to be like to work in a communistic system. Take the case of a surface ship going into overhaul. An overhaul is triggered by age or the condition of equipment. The ship spends a month or so preparing for the shipyard. Once in the shipyard, equipment is replaced, and the deterioration of the ship's structure is repaired. The work involves so much planning and management that each morning there is a meeting between the big wheels of the ship, shipyard personnel and offshore-based naval support personnel. If you want to be entertained while being paid, attend a Navy technical meeting. Some people strive to work catchy buzz-words into the conversation: "symbiotic" "transparency" or "metrics." Then there are the acronym spouters. These are the people who know nothing about the subject but somehow feel that by repeating the abbreviated names of equipment or functions they will be thought of as savvy. It is truly comical.

The ship stays in the yard for three to nine months if everything works out. Usually, there are multiple costs and time overruns, but we are all used to this, so there is no novelty there. The yard has to make the money, so screw the taxpayers if there has to be a choice between people being punished or keeping things under the lid. Now, would you take your car to a garage for routine maintenance and allow yourself to be overcharged for a job that takes longer than estimated and creates problems that did not exist before? What can you say, other than God bless the US Navy and the shipyard people? Where else could you find truer Americans than in an American shipyard, even though the writing on the porta-potty walls makes you wonder what kind of Americans work there?

26. Do Mess with Texas

I am prejudiced against any politician from Texas, along with many of the Texans I have met through the years. The saying, "Don't mess with Texas" may have had some validity at one point, but come on people, America certainly does not need your sleazy politicians. Neither is your past so glorious. You stole some land from the Mexicans and lost miserably at the Alamo, which you now celebrate as if it had been a victory. By the way, how many of you know that Texas was invaded by Pancho Villa, and he got away with it? He got away even after being chased by the US Army and without us declaring war on Mexico.

Anyway, please keep your politicians home in Texas and let them fornicate with the locals instead of screwing America. In case you wonder what I am talking about, remember LBJ. He gave us five years of killing in Vietnam. Imagine if Ross Perot had become president. Would it have been a case of a little Texan Mussolini? John Towers is another Texan who went to Washington. From a Navy master chief, a boatswain mate at that, to the US Senate. Miracles like these can only happen in Texas.

Of course, there were the Bushes. The daddy would almost have been OK if had he stayed at the CIA, where no one would ever find out about his misdeeds. But sending the boy prince, who, like the emperor with no clothes, was not bright enough to sense that he did not belong, was really an insult to the rest of the nation. He got there only after his manipulating thugs stole the election. What is there to brag about? Naming a company Arbusto and then bankrupting it (arbusto is the Spanish word for bush) apparently makes him an achiever and an experienced manager in Texas. Great, but why did you have to let him out of the state? They should feel a bit more obligation to America than they do to Texas.

Now, as if your cesspools have been cleansed again and you need a dumping ground, we wind up with Cruz. Have you ever heard about the big fish in the little pond? In reality you'll have nothing more than little fish in little ponds with inflated egos. Welcome to Texas thinking. You could do America a big favor and keep your trash.

But I love Texas women. I remember Jean, the best ever, who was in my life when I was in my twenties. She had a beautiful set of breasts that moved like gentle waves in a turbulent sea when we had sex. See, I am not against everything from Texas.

27. Poor People are Poor by Choice

Maybe I am an American and I did not even know it. In America, you really cannot disrespect rich people. It is poor people who get the brunt of disdain in America. I was poor in Italy. We were so poor that mom would make one of us see how many eggs we were going to get that day. One of us children had to stick one finger up the ass of the chicken to see if there was an egg ready to come out that day. One morning I forgot to wash my fingers, and as I bit my nails in class, I tasted chicken shit. That is how poor we were. I remember being called a *contadino*, which meant "dirt farmer," and being called other names for having patched clothing. Now, I am just like the Americans I know because I too act as if I were rich, and those who are not richer than I must be deserving of their poverty.

28. Racism is Passed on by the Elders

In Italy, I had no occasion to love or hate black people. During my youth there, I saw one black African. He had set up a stand in front of our school and was selling ginger roots as a teeth whitener. He had a perfect set of teeth. Within six months of trying to be an American, I knew that we were called WOPs by the WASPs and that the blacks were called *mulignami* by the Italians. The noun "eggplant" is *melinzana* in Italian, but in our dialect it is called *mulignama*. So, the American blacks were black on the outside but white like us on the inside; ergo, *mulignami*. Of course, I learned all of the other bad things said about American blacks.

In 1959, I was tired of being in a math class for dummies, so I tried to get into an algebra class. I went to see Mrs. Johnson. She had substituted for one period of the math class I was in, and I liked her. I told her that I wanted to take algebra, and she gave me the algebra book and told me how many chapters I had to learn to take the midterm exams around Christmas. I took the book, did the studying, and aced the test. She got me into her regular class. The next year, my senior year at Long Island City High School, I took geometry and trigonometry, and I felt that I had learned something in school. Mrs. Johnson was black and in my 17 years of life until that point, she was the only human being who showed faith in me.

On the morning of April 5, 1968, I was at my desk in an air-conditioned building that contained all the electronic shops for the 366th AEMS people at Danang, SVN. It was just me and Staff Sergeant Harris, the squadron clerk. We were both typing, sitting in such a way that we were near each other but not able to see each other. Above the din of those manual typewriters he said, "Do you know that Martin Luther King was killed?" Without turning or missing a key stroke I replied, "One less to worry about."

As soon as the words reached my mind, I knew I had done a great wrong. I apologized profusely to him but he didn't accept my apology. His very black and unshaven face showed more disbelief than I had ever seen. I put my helmet and flack vest on and went for a walk. I walked around the base, oblivious to the world around me, thinking about how I had become such a hateful racist.

That day was the beginning of a new me. I knew I had become as American as I was ever going to be, but I also began to question what kind of human being I was. I had given up on Italians within three months of coming to America because of all of their ways of covering their true selves. I had given up on religion when I was 14 years old so I could decide to be what I wanted to be. Up to that day in 1968, I had believed that the Americans were better than Italians because they knew everything and did everything right and, most importantly, were straightforward. But that day, I had done a great wrong while I was being the best American I could be. Eventually Staff Sergeant Harris started talking to me again, but our relationship never returned to normal.

In April 1971, in a place called Long Thanh, SVN, I was drinking a beer in a gazebo while an army warrant officer lifted weights. He flew for the 146th Aviation Company, and I worked on equipment on those planes. He was a reformed drunk who had found God. He was in Vietnam for his third tour as a fixed-wing pilot. He gave me a small hometown newspaper from somewhere in Georgia. He pointed out what he wanted me to read. It was a short article about black people not being able to think because their cranial hairs were not hollow. Since the hair was solid, the brains could not be cooled and would overheat. Simple logic for simple minds.

I looked at him and said it was bullshit and left my beer unfinished, which was a truly sacrilegious act for me, and went back to my hootch thinking that I wasn't the racist of a few years earlier. Looking back, that fellow became my stereotypical redneck, even to this day. It has been more than 46 years, but I cannot erase that horrible time of my life. To this day, I would like to blame the environment of the time that made me that way, but I know that I was 25 years old at the time and should have known better. I could use that worn and abused American redemptive phrase that we use when we try to turn manure into virtue and say that some of my best friends are black.

But I am a better American and better human than that. I do deal with African Americans with extra care and concern and try my best to be helpful. In a sense, that too is discriminatory. I sense that the majority of white Americans are nothing more than taciturn racists; that, I am not. I also have hundreds of acquaintances but no friends, so I really cannot say that some of my best friends are black.

Mrs. Johnson, perhaps you see that you did much more for me than you know, regardless of my slapping you in the face with my words. Yes, I cannot erase that horrible day in Vietnam, but if it had not been for you, I would have never become an engineer, and I would have never been in Vietnam to say such a horrible thing. Instead, I would have been an Italian immigrant living in Queens, New York, saying demeaning things with *gli paesani* about American blacks, Chinese or whatever group that was the current target of my friends. Mrs. Johnson and all black Americans, I am sorry for what I did.

29. The US Navy, Still Opting for the Past

Here are some numbers and little known facts about our glorious US Navy, as of the fall of 2013:

The Navy has 216 admirals and 286 ships that can be deployed, so one admiral controls 1.3 ships.

The Navy has 53,580 officers and 265,901 enlisted, so one officer commands five enlisted.

The Navy, like all US military, has a structured rank system with ten layers of officers and nine layers of enlisted. The enlisted are also subdivided into workers and leaders, with roughly six layers of workers and three layers of noncommissioned officers. Therefore, the US Navy has 13 layers of leaders and six layers of workers. Is this a bit too much leadership or what?

More interesting things about the Navy:

When a big oil tanker comes into a port, you usually see less than half a dozen people handling the ropes used to dock the ship. When a Navy destroyer, which is about 500 feet long, comes into port, you will see at least 60 sailors handling ropes on the ship and at least a dozen more on the pier. Most of the sailors inside the ship are at watch stations.

When a Navy ship leaves or enters a port there is a period of time where all propulsion engines are put online for two to three hours or more. The ship is obligated to maintain speeds less than 11KTS in channels, but yet they use four jet engines to achieve this speed. Even though with a single engine spinning one propeller the ship can achieve 17KTS or more. Furthermore the control systems to start and stop those engines can start another engine in 40 seconds or so and have its power applied to the shaft. Jet engines are fuel guzzlers. One of these ships under full power uses over 100 gallons of fuel per minute. I put in a beneficial suggestion to get them to arrive and depart port with one engine per shaft and the other two in standby, and it was rejected. That was at least 20 years ago, and it would have saved much fuel and engine wear and tear. Reason is not applied if someone else is paying for the gas.

The Navy has names for each layer of its ranks. At the beginning, the enlisted sailors are called seamen and then become petty officers. The highest rank in this sequence is Master Chief Petty Officer. Every one of the almost 400,000 people in the Navy knows that petty means small. It has always meant small. So why would you want to address the highest ranked enlisted with three laudable adjectives and a pejorative one? A little logic would make these people abandon this crap and go to the same ranking names as the other branches of the US military. No one could ridicule the title Sergeant Major.

The Navy has much tradition, and though it has ships with nuclear power plants and can launch airplanes from aircraft carriers, the Navy tends to adhere to the past as if it were truly relevant today. Take the indoctrination process of the petty officer first class who was promoted to become a CPO, an unwritten, unauthorized, but tolerated process that lasts a couple of months. The day after the list announcing the advancement of first class petty officers to CPO, the selectees begin to wear name tags with the words "Chief Selectee." He or she carriers a wooden box at all times with the insignias of the three CPO ranks and undergoes special training conducted by the shipboard CPOs. He or she organizes cookouts or other events to raise money for a big celebration at the end of this period. Those parties used to resemble a frat party, with hazing and lots of drinking. I don't know what it's like today. The next day, the petty officer becomes a chief petty officer, or in the local lingo, a member of the goat locker. At the end of this initiation into chiefdom, all of the newly minted chiefs are sent to a school on how to be leaders.

30. Not for Degreed Engineers

Federal civil service rules, as applied in Norfolk, Va., are very unfair to graduate engineers. The only way to get more money is to go into management. This creates dead ends for good engineers when they are 30 to 50 years old. The outfit I worked for had many graduate engineers. Some of these people were registered professional engineers and some had advanced degrees in engineering. The best of these engineers were the center of knowledge in the groups they worked in. Even I was considered to be a good engineer when I worked there.

Sometimes, we would get calls from ships with problems wondering whether they could still get underway. We helped them and sometimes even advised them not to go. We were all GS12s with no hope of advancement. Even if we had reached that rank early in our careers and had 10 to 20 more years before retirement, we were resigned to being GS12s. There were ex–Navy chiefs who upon retirement would come to work for us first as contractors and then would be hired as G9s or GS11s. In less than five years, these fellows would be promoted to GS12. They had no degrees and often no grasp of engineering, but they did have a bag of tricks and tried to fit the symptoms of new problems into one of the tricks that had solved a problem for them before.

Most of these people did not know such basics as the law of conservation of energy, but they were GS12s just like the engineers with state registration. Some of these engineers would try management, the only way to get to the GS13 level. Some would acknowledge their mistake of having hired on with the wrong employer, but age and the new challenges of the work made them stay until they retired. A few misfits would return to GS12 after figuring out that engineering was their calling. I went through that process a long time ago.

If you were to look into how many GS13s without degrees there are, you would be surprised. Here is how they make GS13s in Norfolk, VA. If you were a good boy and made the right connections and kissed all of the rings, you would be promoted with your mentor. In my old place of work, if you had been a good little soldier and you had three years to retire, you would be promoted to a GS13 as the supervisor of a group of people working on similar equipment. That way, you went home with hundreds of dollars more in monthly retirement.

If you were a good-looking woman, you would easily make it to GS13 with only a high school diploma. Later, degreed female engineers started coming on the scene and their very presence began to establish a fairer practice of how women were promoted. But we had a GS13 who somehow also had the duties as the social coordinator for the outfit. One year for the Fourth of July command picnic, she solicited people for the watermelon seed-spitting contest. We made GS12 pay and could stop a warship from going to sea, but this lady organized picnics as a GS13. God bless the Navy.

Now, my old employer has facility managers and liaison people as GS13s, as well as those being rewarded for past favors or obedience above the call of duty. But those engineers who make things happen and save the Navy millions of dollars yearly by preventing uneducated money wasting *try this and see what happens* methods of defining and fixing problems, these engineers cannot be advanced to GS13 and be paid their worth. Blessed be the civil service managers and administrators in the Norfolk area civil service system, for they know who their friends are.

31. Israel Is Dearer to America than Any of Our 50 States

The most un-American thing that has been happening for almost 70 years is our limitless and no-questions-asked support of Israel. I doubt there is an American state that has received more assistance from the US government than Israel. Once the Israelis obtained a territory to claim as their own from the UN, they began grabbing land in a way that made the American doctrine of manifest destiny seem amateurish. Remember your American history? The Native Americans were savages, we needed the land and God was on our side. The Arabs were unable to grow trees, roses and peppers in the desert, but the Israelis can with the help of the Jewish God. After all, God made the Jews, then the Christians, and then the Muslims; presently, he has been experimenting with American evangelists. Of course, he is partial to the Jews. What mother doesn't love her first son more than anyone else in the brood? In reality, I doubt that any man or god really gives a shit about humans. But since the Jewish settlers in the Palestinian lands claim that God told them to go steal land, I had to say that.

Americans, the people who try so hard to convince the world that freedom—including freedom of religion—is important, do not talk about the simple fact that to be an Israeli citizen one must be a Jew. This means that America is supporting a theocracy. Since Israel took over Palestine, America has had a schizophrenic foreign policy. If Israel occupies or takes over land, it is OK. If Russia occupies Afghanistan, or Iraq takes over Kuwait, that is not OK.

If we attempt to get Israel to make peace and allow whatever portion of Palestine is still Palestinian to be a sovereign land, the Israelis publicly go along with the charade. At the last minute, they put up fences here and there or build hundreds of housing units to force the pursuers of peace to move away from the peace table. This has been going on for almost 50 years now, and it will continue until Palestine is but a historical footnote. I believe there will be a day when Israel will be building housing units in St. Peter's Square, and America will still ask for peace while allowing Israel to be the vagabond and bully of the Middle East.

The American Jews, who are as numerous as the Jews in Israel, disseminate pro-Israeli propaganda that is tolerated as if it were another American institution. In case you don't follow, there is a major movie release about every two years that involves Jews and the Holocaust. Rarely does anyone make movies about the lives of the Palestinians in the occupied lands. I guess Hollywood is afraid to go there, or perhaps they cannot get visas. On television, documentaries about the Holocaust run monthly. Newspapers carry frequent articles about Holocaust survivors. In America, we have problems getting people to accept a mosque in their community, yet there was no resistance to building the Holocaust Museum so close to American historical buildings in Washington, D.C.

Why are there Holocaust museums in more American cities than there are in Israel?

Why isn't there a single Native American museum in Israel?

Why isn't there a single African American museum in Israel?

Why isn't there a museum in Israel for those killed on the US Liberty Ship by Israeli attacks?

Why isn't there a single museum in America for the millions of Asians killed by nature and world leaders or a museum for those killed by Stalin?

Why isn't there a single museum in Israel or America for the Polish intelligentsia killed by the NKVD during World War II?

Why is it that though Israel claims to be our friend, they have been spying on America since the inception of Israel?

I believe the answer to all of these questions is simply that the Jews are sophisticated thinkers, well-organized and focused on achieving their goals. I also believe that the endless persecution of the Jews, probably by every society that they tried to live with, while strengthening their beliefs, has instilled in them the idea that it is only a matter of time before a new group will rise and slaughter them as if they were animals. But someplace, sometime, somebody should emerge from Israel saying, "We got enough land, we got enough safety, we have slaughtered our neighbors on a 10-to-1 ratio in every war, so maybe we can get along without so much blood and greed."

If that doesn't happen, then watch out. A few thousand years later, the pope will be Jewish, as was intended from the beginning. After all, wasn't Jesus a Jew? When this happens, will the people believe that the Second Coming has occurred? And occurred in Rome, not in Jerusalem, because Rome is a heck of a lot more urban, and there is better food in Rome than I have ever had in Israel. And a roman pine tree is a hell of lot more majestic than the equivalent cedars of Lebanon.

32. Reap What You Sowed

If it weren't for their religion, which most of us know little about, we would hate the Muslim people just because they are different. We are, after all, a gathering of humans for whom hate is a way of life. But there are reasons to hate Arabs, just as the Arabs have reasons to hate us, so we are even. After all, they even kill each other. Of course, in America we are truly good and loving people, despite the 30,000 or 80 000(?) yearly gun fatalities. Sarcasm aside, tries to find an incident in which America has treated Arabic people fairly. Our support of any government is based entirely on whether we can get our oil and use a country for our military bases. So they get a Nasser or Mubarak, a Shah or a Khomeini, an Assam or Bashar Al-Assad. It doesn't matter to us as long as the oil flows our way and we can kill Muslims from bases in other Muslim countries that need our money. This has been our diplomatic attitude toward a billion people.

Do we deserve the attacks that some people from these countries have mounted on us? Yes. We screwed the natives by dealing with their dictators. We supported Israel regardless of whether it acted rightly or wrongly. They are paying us back, nothing more, nothing less. Therefore, their acts of rebellion should not be called terrorism. Sending a drone or plane thousands of miles away to kill indiscriminately is much less courageous than invading the land of the enemy to bring death and destruction. Just because our bureaucratic intelligence agencies and our military, always trained for the last but not the present battle, cannot handle new ways of killing does not make these people terrorists. They are fighters for a cause, whereas our fighters are confused ex–hamburger flippers who wonder why the hell they are there.

Maybe in 100 years this phase will pass, but until then, things will worsen for us in America. The TSA people in charge of airport security will progress to the phase of sticking gloved fingers up our anuses, and because we are good Americans we will undergo it because it is good for America. The spy agencies will monitor our thoughts and imprison us for thinking, and we will keep on sending politically appointed ambassadors who do not know the language to insult the natives. The terrorists will keep on killing, and their mothers, like the mothers of the dead American heroes, will cry. The killing will go on, the movies will be made, and the mothers will cry. All of this is happening under the domain of the same god, whether we call him Jehovah, God or Allah. What else can be said about us, except that we are fools who kill and maim through ignorance and then invoke invented gods?

33. He Is a WASP, Tall and Presidential

In America, we have a penchant for studying the qualifications of people who deal with important things. Our medical people have college degrees, state licenses and exorbitant insurance fees. If a doctor is poorly trained or incompetent, he or she can mess up the lives of up to 10,000 patients during a lifetime of medical practice. But when it comes to choosing leaders, the only important qualification is whether the candidate is tall, good-looking and personable. No schooling required. Sadly, no voter training is required either so that the voters could decipher what the sleazy, but photogenic, politicians are saying. And this is democracy.

34. The National Beauty Contest

Why don't I vote? In 1969, I voted for Nixon because he had a plan to end the war in Vietnam. The bastard didn't tell anyone that he was first going to kill another 20,000 poor sons of bitches there. I promised myself not to do it again. I broke my promise and voted for Reagan in 1984. I was so mad at my wife that I promised to nullify her vote. I did, and we both lost. Then in 2004, I voted for Kerry because he ran against the boy with no brains from Texas. So I voted three times and failed three times.

Should there be a law mandating that I must vote, I will, but until then I think American elections are a beauty contest sponsored by the rich, and I would rather not participate. I really don't give a shit about the cliché that asks what would happen if everybody felt the same way. If everyone did feel the same way, there would still be some sons of bitches pushing another idiot upon us. I feel that the best human product is stupidity. Why else do we repeat the saying that prostitution was the first profession? What if the man who hired the whore paid for it by giving her a lamb or a basket of fruit? Was he not a shepherd or a farmer? If he was, then wasn't he a professional? Simply stated, voting and democracy are the best things that happened to humanity. Now if we could just develop humans who think.

35. American Schools

When I was young, the smartest people in the world were teachers. As I got older and had dealings with teachers, I find American teachers are the most unimaginative, robotic humans that could ever be put in a classroom. They start out with conviction, but the most bureaucratic system of management in the world kills that zeal. Then you are left with robots waiting for retirement. The fact that a trash man makes more money than a teacher may also have something to do with it. Don't forget that in America, the country of fairness and equality, 75 percent of our teachers are female, and only 25 percent of the principals are females. God bless American fairness.

36. Virginia Interstates, a Work in Progress

I am now 70 years old, and I drive fifty miles to work and then the same to return home, five days a week on I-64 in the Hampton

Roads area. I have noticed that the transportation and state police department here have the wrong concept of how to keep traffic moving. Road work is done during the day when road usage is highest. This causes traffic slowdowns, much waste in energy and much more pollution. There is a tunnel I must use every day, and the transportation department has found all kinds of ways to close it. It seems that in southeastern Virginia, we have the only interstate tunnel in the world, and the natives are still learning how to maximize its usage after almost 50 years. There goes another waste of fuel and unnecessary pollution.

Then there are our illustrious State Police, who at the scene of accidents create unnecessary traffic jams as if each accident is the first they've ever responded to. Though it is a merciful concept to provide care to the injured, there is a higher social obligation to keep the traffic going. In each accident, there are those who caused the accident and those who suffered its consequences. But there are also several hundred people like me who really don't care and just want to get to our destinations.

Why not train these troopers to quickly document the scene with video and photos? These could be used by insurance companies and courts. Fire trucks could then push aside the inoperable vehicles and clear the way for the remainder of the people on the road. Cruel and inconsiderate? Try to estimate the damage you are doing to the environment and passing on to your replacements when 500 engines insides 500 vehicles inch along and cover one mile in ten minutes. How hurtful is that? And what has each driver done to deserve the delays and waste?

37. No, I Do Not Discriminate—Just Ask Me

Once upon a time, there was a truly evil man who came up with the idea of creating an Aryan race. He was a horrible man, and I don't know why no one has used him on a pro-abortion banner. The world rebelled against that concept and life went on, but I am a bit confused. What is womanhood doing when it mates only with taller males? Or what is a lesbian or gay couple doing when they go to the sperm bank and ask for blond, tall, smart sperm?

38. The Beginning of a Bad Thing

In 1966 while I still in school, my classmate Ziggy became the first political activist that I had known. Ziggy would try to convince everyone that Reagan was the savior of California. He approached me once and quickly figured out that I did not like Reagan or politics. To his credit, he left me alone thereafter, but the conviction and vigor with which he defended everything Republican awakened my Italian cynicism.

In time I started to pay attention to politics because so many people and so much time are spent on it. Somehow, I begin to dislike, and even hate, Republicans because I believe that many of them are just closet haters of anything that is not as they believe. The hate shows itself in arguments when these poor uneducated and uncivil bastards struggle so hard to hide their hate of African Americans. Most of the time, you hear that all welfare recipients are black or that black women raise children from multiple fathers. My attitude toward republicans/ conservatives was formed mostly on the basis of what I had seen in the US military, where true American scum hides under the shield of defending America.

Then again, the US military may not be the only hiding place for racial bigots. After all, the Republicans were once the people who elected Lincoln and stopped slavery. It's so sad that by the time LBJ got his wish with the Civil Rights Act of 1964, so many Southern Democrats switched sides and made the South go red. In so doing they showed their true feelings of hatred for everything different from themselves. They really didn't switch sides but just got off a train that had switched tracks.

Here are some observations about those American reds, who claim to be the true protectors of America. In the 1960s they gave us Nixon, the crook. Spiro was credited as the coiner of some now-forgotten sleaze, and he did become the effete snob that he accused others of being. By the way, I have never heard anyone paint Agnew's Greek heritage in a negative light. Are Americans of Greek ancestries above the normal xenophobic hate that true Americans dish out for all other ethnic groups?

Then came Ford, a nice human being, who conveniently pardoned Nixon before he was even charged with anything. The intent was good, but Ford would have been impeached had he and Nixon been Democrats. To this day, no Republican will say that Nixon was a stupid bastard, and Ford did well in pardoning him. I would think that being reasonable means that you don't shy away from facts, even if it means shattering some of your beliefs. Ford was an accidentally decent Republican, but he didn't last long.

A couple of years later, Carter pardoned all the misdeeds that some Vietnam soldiers and draft dodgers had committed. This was unacceptable to the Republicans, and they cried bloody murder. The military of the time hated Carter for that, but he also did not increase the pay of the military, and supposedly there were cases of active duty personnel using food stamps. Money can obscure true feelings.

Next came Lee Atwater, the American version of Joseph Goebbels. Lee, a good Southern boy, produced the semen that has grown into the hateful politics that are destroying the GOP. In simple English, he might have had nurturing parents, but he sure grew up to be a mean bastard. He lied, cheated and helped some otherwise useless politicians get elected. The way he did it became a standard operating procedure for the GOP, and to this day the Republicans would rather spread manure than act like reasonable humans. At his death bed, he sent letters of repentance to those whom he ruined. Hey Lee, how are you doing down there? Is it as hot as they say it is? Have you found all your friends yet?

Let me explain American repentance. When I was 14 years old, I gave up on religion, a decision that I am still very proud of. A few years back, an old geezer in a hardware store was bragging about being a reborn Christian. He looked at me and asked if I was born again. I replied that I never fucked up my life to the point where I had to be reborn. I rarely say the right thing at the right time, but that morning I did, and I still feel good about it. Everybody within earshot went quiet.

One of the human behaviors I both fear and hate most is when a human errs in his ways and continues to do so until death or a long prison term convinces this person to repent. Then the bastard turns to God and feels that by apologizing all will be well. Bullshit. You were a loser when you did evil things, and you are still a loser once you proclaim that God saved you. Evil is never really erased like a dry-erase board. Evil messes people up, and you should pay a much higher price than proclaiming yourself a godly idiot and forgetting it all. Lee Atwater was an evil man, and his acts of hateful ignorance followed by godly repentance hurt America.

Then the country got Reagan, the B-movie actor who was barely a B-movie actor even in the eyes of Hollywood. Oh, I take it back; he was a Hollywood war hero who made training films for our side while still going home at night. Must have been tough. I wonder if Reagan ever had the balls to buddy up with Jimmy Stewart and talk about doing his part for the war effort. In case you don't know, Stewart was a combat pilot and flew actual B17 bombing missions over Germany, as did Clark Gable.

Reagan was a Democrat who was swayed into the GOP by his first wife. Jane Wyman convinced him to be a Republican, and Nancy convinced him to blacklist some actors while he was president of the Screen Actors Guild. Bless him, a poor actor in a role too big for him. With Reagan in the White House, a new American way of thinking was born. If Ronnie screws up, it is OK. Gosh he is old, and Nancy was most likely to blame because she didn't understand what the astrologist told her to do. To me, the Reagan people were low-class hoods who would have never survived the politics of NYC.

Reagan was in charge when 241 US soldiers were killed in Beirut, and 13 more died later because the US Marines guarding the gate had empty guns. Reagan gave America that great loss, and this is never brought up when the small minds that think of Ronnie as a guide to all that needs to be done in America bring up the mistakes of subsequent Democratic leaders. Years later, Clinton gets a blow job in the oval office and lies about it, and the entire GOP wants impeachment. You stupid sons of bitches. You mean to say that there is more evil in getting blow jobs in the oval office and lying about it than in allowing 254 Americans to be killed because the guards had guns without bullets?

There were other issues that show Reagan was not even a tenth of the president that some believe him to be. Look up debategate, lobbying scandal, EPA scandal or Inslaw scandal for a few examples. Consider the treasonous event in which his people talked to the Iranians about the hostages they were holding, prior to his taking office from Carter. This was staged so that the B-movie actor could commence his stewardship of America like a triumphant Caesar entering Rome. It was Hollywood at its best and treason at its truest.

Reagan claimed ignorance during the trials of the Iran-Contra missile deal, in which Oliver North and his leaders sold missiles to Iran and used part of the money to give bullets to the Contras in Nicaragua. The planes that had carried the arms were then filled with drugs so that the CIA could sell the cocaine back home. Ollie, the Vietnam War hero, was there, but he knew nothing about it. A typical military mind at work – victory has a thousand fathers, but defeat is a bastard. Only in America is there a legal system in which Ollie, the only Vietnam hero in America, gets to go around in his bus selling his crap to idiots who have no sense of history. The SOB was sentenced by a court and walked away on a technicality.

During Reagan's two terms, we got an F president who had more White House aides indicted than ever before or since. Here are some names that you should know if you think you know American History:

1. Lyn Nofziger
2. Michael Deaver
3. James Watt
4. John Poindexter
5. Richard Secord
6. Elliott Abrams
7. Robert C. McFarlane
8. Alan D. Fiers Jr.
9. Thomas G. Clines
10. Carl R. Channell
11. Richard R. Miller
12. Frank D. Gomez
13. Donald Fortier
14. Clair George
15. Rita Lavelle
16. Philip Winn

17. Thomas Demery
18. Deborah Gore Dean
19. Catalina Villaponda
20. Joseph A. Strauss
21. Oliver North

Oh, the worshipping of Ronnie never deals with the simple fact that the moron took away laws that prevented greedy people from devastating the financial system. Voilà, the American taxpayers had to shell out $160 billion to pay for the money lost during the savings and loan debacle. To think that there are people around who actually think that Reagan brought down Communism. You've got to be kidding. Poland was the weakest link in the communist bloc. Even in the 1960s, the US government tried to find ways to help the divorce, but nothing was done. There were many Polish citizens who died trying to free Poland before Reagan became president. Look into it, and stop hogging victories that were not achieved by your demented thespian.

Ziggy, I hope you are still around. Your eagerness in pushing your idiot idol so long ago made you responsible for screwing up America. If you did ever achieve some logical thinking, what does it feel like to have been so stupid back then? I know the feeling, because for at least 55 years of my life, I obeyed my pecker. Still, I think I have done less damage than you have. I bet that you have become another reborn Christian.

39. The Kids Today Suck

About 2,400 years ago, an older man supposedly said:

> The children now love luxury; they have bad manners, contempt for authority; they show disrespect for elders and love chatter in place of exercise. Children are now tyrants, not the servants of their households. They no longer rise when elders enter the room. They contradict their parents, chatter before company, gobble up dainties at the table, cross their legs, and tyrannize their teachers.

This saying is attributed to great men of other eras as well, and I have heard older people say the same thing throughout my life. Now, I hear people younger than I am say the same thing.

Now that I am old, the only thing I can say is that old people tend to exaggerate their earlier times for no reason other than to sound experienced. Kids today call what dangles between their legs a penis and not some other cute name as we did when we were kids. They tell their parents that they love them. They obey just as much as they did 2,400 years ago, and they have ten times more problems than the accusing old men handled. If you are an old fart and you think otherwise, don't say it. At best it makes you a silly human who is not even smart enough to understand that you failed your offspring, if they are such lousy human beings. If the world remained as you think it was when you were young, women would feel too shameful to report rape, mobs would lynch African Americans with impunity, drunk drivers would go unpunished and child molesters would not be brought to justice. Those who claim that yesterday was a better day are fooling themselves.

40. Not an American Yet

Who am I? As stated elsewhere, after arriving in America, I decided to shed everything Italian and become an American. On November 22, 1963, I was sitting in a classroom at the Academy of Aeronautics waiting for the next class to start when a classmate returned from smoking and said that JFK had been shot. I still remember watching replays of it on TV in Astoria, later that day.

During the weekend I worked at the Astoria Manor as a dishwasher and janitor from midnight on Friday to noon on Sunday. That night, my Italian-American supervisor's first words to me were: "Tony, I was so glad that the fellow who shot JFK did not have an Italian surname." I did not understand what he was saying, but he explained that if the killer had been Italian, there would be retribution against Americans with Italian names. I did not believe it.

As time went on and I got to be more American, those words stuck with me, as did the fact that Armando had come to America as an

8-year-old boy, and was later drafted into the army, where he commanded an American tank in Africa, Italy, France and Germany. Why would he be afraid of having an Italian name? As my Americanization continued, I started getting pissed when dumb Americans would make fun of Italians by aiming their jokes at me. They would make fun of my heritage only after they figured out that I was Italian. Then, there were the people who always had to come up with some association with Italy. For example:

"Hey, Tony, where you from?"

"I was born and raised in Italy."

"I was there once and blah blah blah."

"My sister-in-law is Eyetalian and, boy, can she cook!"

And tens of other superficial observations that are routinely made by people who know so little, yet they feel like the big fish in the big pond, regardless.

As time went on, I realized many Americans were small-minded people who wanted to deport everyone who had committed even the smallest crime. My supervisor may have been right. In case you don't know, there is a place in the US Constitution where it says that you cannot punish people for blood crimes. That means that if the daddy does something bad, you cannot punish the children. After the shameful events of September 11, we wound up with so much xenophobic news reporting that any individual with an Arabic surname was automatically guilty of the crime. This added fuel to the fire for the small minded.

In April 2003 I was on a flight to Frankfurt, Germany. The lady sitting next to me was an American citizen who had been born in Egypt but educated in America. She was a professor. We started talking about all of the things that make short and mostly forgettable conversations in airplanes, but then she told me this story. Sometime in 2002 or 2003, someone went into the Los Angeles International Airport and either fired a gun or somehow caused problems. The fellow was of Arabic descent. The lady said: "As soon as I heard the story on the radio, I knew the FBI was going to come knocking on the door and asking us questions. They had done it before."

When you use the term "melting pot" to refer to the way aliens are treated in America, believe me when I tell you that it is bullshit. In America, I am not an American. I am an Italian-American. This is also an issue when I go to Italy. As soon as the taxi drivers detect any hesitation in coming up with the right Italian word, those sons of bitches say, "*Oh, ma tu sei Italo Americano?*" Oh, but you are Italian-American? Where and when am I going to be a non- hyphenated resident of a country? In case you feel yourself to be superior to people not born here who have come to partake of the American bounty, here is a little truism: Your mom spread her legs, you popped out, you grew up, and Bingo, you are a born-in-America guy. Whoopee. Whereas I and millions of others voluntarily took a test to attain your self-glorified citizenship status. I passed the test. I have been to wars for this country without wearing a uniform. I can speak three languages. I know the ways of other lands. I know more about America than you will ever know, and the reason I progressed was simply due to having more drive than your lazy-ass way of life helped you cultivate.

If you and I had started out in an achievement race, you would have lost miserably. In case you don't get it, decades or centuries ago your great-great-grandpa was just like me. If he could come back, he would be ashamed of you and your clannish and xenophobic ways.

41. Screw You, Third World

I believe that the majority of people on Earth live in nations with lower living standards than we have in America because in those areas, corruption, religion and traditions are more prevalent. In North America and northern Europe, there is less corruption, less tradition and less religious domination than the rest of the world, and there are better governments because of that. Communist countries, if China and Cuba are really communist countries, may have less religious domination, but they have more corruption. Corruption and religion are parasites like kudzu, that strangler of all flora on the side of American roads. It is those parasites that hold back advancement of the natives.

In all of Africa, Southeast Asia and Central and South America, corrupt governments, traditions that established the moneyed people as superior to others, and churches that advise the poor to have more children even though there is no food for them, have created backward countries. Because of the inhumane treatment of the masses, revolutions and terrorism are prevalent. Imagine penned animals without food, and you understand the majority of humanity in those countries. Yet the United Nation sits there, and like a doctor without medicine or facilities, looks at these problems, writes them down and keeps thinking that it is doing the best that it can. And the natives suffer and die, and the religious say prayers and the rich are too busy to help.

42. I Am Blessed

This one really bugs me. Early in the morning, I go for coffee at a convenience store, and the minimum wage clerk, as a departing salutation says, "Have a blessed day." I take it as an insult but keep quiet about it. She has no power to bless me and her God is her God. I used to hear *"Dio ti benedica"* as a kid, but I don't think that God ever blessed me. I owe thanks to the thousands of humans who have helped me, but none to God. When I think of God, I think of many things, all of them negative. For example, religious humans are so proud that God gave them such a wonderful body, but the body is actually poorly designed. The symptoms of acid reflux, for example, make people think they are having a heart attack.

That, however, is a rather childish example when contrasted with the fact that your God, according to you, gave humans an insatiable sex drive but solved the problem of sewage disposal by putting the vagina between the piss and shit holes. If a civil engineer ever did that, he would be fired. Then again, if you look at the positioning of sexual organs in the avian world, you would probably kneel and thank your poor engineer of a god. Thanks to our evolution, we have managed to play in these bacterially infested sewage disposal areas from the beginning, and –guess what? – we have even created medicine to cure the infections we get from such pleasures. Therefore, being blessed by another human is an insult. When I was a believer, I did pray, but to this day I can honestly say I never got an answer.

43. American English

The English language is a good language. In my native language, we say "fuck you" by saying "*Vai a Ha Fare in Culo,*" the literal translation of which is "go do it in the ass." English says the same thing with such authoritative brevity that those two words stop the listeners. But English isn't always so perfect. When one says "climb down," he is being illogical but grammatically correct. How can that be? Or take the word sewer, which describes where the poo-poo goes but also means someone who works with cloth. And when you say "what a smart ass," are you describing an ass that hurts or an intelligent guy? When you reiterate something, are you really re-repeating it? Of course there are a few other words that come to mind such as lead, decimate, and sit up, friendly fire.

Everybody knows what a short circuit is, and few understand that the English words do not describe the fact. There is no such a thing as a short circuit. A circuit does not decrease in length when it malfunctions in a certain way. It does decrease its resistance to the flow of current. There's nothing long or short about that. And an open circuit is also impossible. If it is a circuit, it is closed.

There are also those who want to create new words out of laziness, especially down here in southeastern Virginia. The local journalists have tried for years to establish "nor'easter" or "nor eastern" as a new word. Why don't the morons stick with northeastern, a word that is used by the rest of the nation and the English-speaking world? Is it because they think that it is cute to generate another word variation on a language that has already birthed so many words with incestuous roots? These are the same people who say "ideer" instead of idea, and "impotant" instead of important.

How can English get any respect in the world when we have spelling bees in America? A spelling bee is an admission that English is an illogical aggregation of letters brought about by the laziness of etymologists. Perhaps we should have copied the French by establishing an American equivalent of their *Académie Française*. There is no spelling bee for Italian because each letter is pronounced. So, spelling bees are nothing more than unabashedly admitting that we have a language that you have to memorize. Mathematics is a language, but it has rules, and the rules are always the same whether we enunciate them or just follow them. English could be changed to having a logical form and make us all seem more intelligent.

44. It Was His Fault

Autobiographies and memoirs mislead even the most diligent people. Whether the book's subject did the writing himself or had someone else do it, the result is the truth gets exaggerated when it helps the individual and gets overlooked when it demeans the individual. Take the case of Robert M. Gates. He is, according to him, the only American in government who knows right from wrong. Just read his trash. This *cafone* was the expert on the Soviet Union, yet he saw the collapse of the Soviet Union on TV like the rest of the world.

The American government lied to us about the Soviet Union from 1950 to 1991. That country was poor. Even to this day, they don't have paved roads between their major cities. The populace was poor and lived on near-starvation diets. The satellite nations were waiting to break away, but the American government made them our potent adversaries. How many trillions of dollars did that lie cost us? Of course, the government can justify that. They classify everything so that you and I will never know the true ability of the Soviets to invade any country during the Cold War.

Bobby was an expert in heaping manure on the compost pile of governmental lies. He was not smart enough to realize we could not win wars in Iraq or Afghanistan and criticized those who did want us to get out of there. This guy does not understand that it wasn't a good idea to waste trillions of dollars and sacrifice 5,000 dead Americans to kill one man and turn the country into a lawless wasteland. We cannot call our deeds in Iraq good, worthy or admirable. We just set a killing machine in motion in a society that lives by corruption.

So Bobby gets his money from his forgettable book, and like millions of other American government workers who had no problems with their employment while they were there, now he tells all. Bullshit, Bobby. You are a loser who lost sight of reality when you were young and made your career your main goal in life. Now, with a grubby heart, you criticize things you could have changed while you were there. Your nobility is like the other million or so government workers and politicians who lose their sincerity and then exculpate themselves by demeaning other losers. It is like children with dirty diapers castigating the others for smelling shitty. If you had ever held a job where you had to earn an honest buck, you wouldn't have written the book. When you look in the mirror, you should turn the light on and see the real you.

45. Inches Forever

Simple logic here. America exports heavy equipment and military machines to other countries. We make lots of money at this, while China sends us everything else. Go to Walmart and look at any dry product and see its origins. Think about it this way: 6.5 billion people in the world use the metric system, which involves much more than just miles versus kilometers. Americans, however, proudly use our own ridiculous system. Imagine how much time is wasted insuring that the conversion of measurements is correct when sending material to the space station?

46. How Much for a Ride to the Space Station this Week?

At the end of World War II, the occupying Allies gleaned the German war machine for top scientists and the latest war equipment. I don't know if we got the cream of the crop, but we got some good ones. These guys did build our missile systems and space programs. Because we are Americans we have to do things in a big way, so we sent spaceships like Greyhound busses into orbit while the prudent Russians sent little Volkswagens.

Then we ran out of enthusiasm, or money, or both, and we stopped the great search, except for the international space station, which is shared with other countries. To get to the space station, we hire Russians and their equipment to bring people there and back. Where is the American pride? Where is the American know-how? We captured German scientists, and they gave us a space program because they had paid attention to an American by the name of Robert H. Goddard, who, years before WWII, had been shunned by the US military. We spend trillions of dollars on it. It seems that American pride seems to exist only when we are bombing indigent countries; we are at the mercy of the Russians to go to space. God bless America.

47. Salute that Flag

On the Norfolk naval base, there are least ten flagpoles that require the ritual of flag-raising each morning and evening. If you multiply that by 200 or more bases and military installations, you have a five- to ten-minute ceremony being repeated a few thousand times.

Does it make us more patriotic to conduct so many flag-raising ceremonies?

If we are more patriotic, does that explain why we start wars so often or have 2.4 million Americans in jails?

Just wondering.

48. Yes, We Are Authorized to Sell What We Ain't Got

On any Sunday morning, there are religious leaders on TV selling their wares. These people have no civil licenses to do what they are doing. Religion is the selling of products that you don't have, and millions of Americans buy it, as have billions of people throughout the ages.

But it should be different for Americans. Americans routinely buy goods in grocery stores that need to be weighed, and the scales are calibrated yearly. At the gas pumps these same Americans use calibrated pumps. Even at the doctors' offices, the sphygmomanometers used to measure their blood pressure have calibration period of three months. Our populace is so ignorant that it is protected from being cheated at the grocery store, the gas pump, and even at the doctor's office, but this populace embraces anyone that sells God. These same believers can vote, and the vote of such ignorant people counts the same as the vote of educated people. We wonder how American democracy has such a hard time surviving when the politicians we elect are nothing more than copies of the ignorant people who elect them.

49. We Could Solve this Problem if We Cared

The African Americans have a serious problem on their hands. The problem is composed of many little problems, such as:

a. American whites, the Asians, the European immigrants and the Latinos all discriminate against the blacks. If you do not believe me, ask an African American.

b. The African Americans have little family foundation to rely on and be proud of. How else do you explain grandmas raising grandchildren while daughters sort out their lives? I do not know if this is a hereditary thing from the slavery period or a simple "fuck-'em-and leave-'em" syndrome on the part of young black males, who at the sight of a probable new sex mate become total servants to their peckers.

c. Successful blacks have done little to support those still in the ghettos. Successful blacks become just like old-money, white Americans. I got mine. Screw you.

d. The schools, the churches, and other organizations that cater to blacks are staffed with people who do not speak

English and do not understand that the way to success in America is to be better than your competition. Instead, these young blacks are educated in such a way as not even speak the same language as the rest of the country into which they were born and raised. Success for them is mostly a dream. And when these unprepared youths fail, we the whites, the Asians, the Latinos are the first to castigate them.

e. Black Americans, in a sense, are worse off today than they were 100 years ago. One hundred years ago, they lived in misery, they knew it, and they did what they could to survive. Mixing with the successful whites was only while working as household help. Today, with TV showing every aspect of life, and consumptive spending, and daily intermingling with all races of people, the African Americans are put in a position in which they know that on the other side of the fence there is a better way to live. But in a sense, they are still segregated because in their own domiciles they live with poverty and squalor and little hope. They can jump over the unseen social fence that separates us from them and do menial jobs for minimal wages. At the end of their shifts, they may stop and buy things in stores that white people or other non-African American own, but the rest of the time the African Americans, like untethered animals that return to the barns at dusk, return to their ghettos, and Americans accept this as normal. And in a hundred years this problem will also be looked at, and maybe solved. And thank you, you sneaky American Democracy for not having any deadlines on when all of the concepts of democracy will apply to all of the people, all of the time.

f. Discrimination in America is alive and well and it is accomplished by many means. In NYC, if you want to move into an expensive apartment building there is an association that qualifies you. How many African Americans live in those luxury buildings? In Williamsburg, Virginia, there is presently a 12 percent or higher unemployment rate. But our city government and social leaders see nothing wrong with importing young workers from Eastern Europe, instead of helping local black kids break the cycle of poverty.

g. Some of the worst problems that African Americans face are self-inflicted. The idea that black people, but not white people, can use the word "nigger" when talking about themselves makes the black Americans that adhere to that thinking rather stupid. How can you pay a singer, a comic or other entertainer to use such a word, but then be offended when a non-black person uses it? Don't you see the lack of logic there?

Some or most of these problems can only be solved by African Americans themselves. If the many caring and willing black people who try so hard to break the chains of black poverty were able to unite, it would be a start. But because black Americans act just like white Americans when it comes to solving problems that may take time or money, the cycle of poor education, killing of the young, unemployment, death, prison and menial and minimum wage part-time work will be their future. And to think that so many Americans are Christians and on Sunday they pray to their god, and are lauded as good Christians for sharing.

Perhaps American black youths ought to be mentored by the legal/illegal Latinos. Stereotypically, these are people who leave their native communities and come here to clean our commodes or cut the grass and be treated like the stuff flushed down a commode. Yet they send money to their families. They also keep their language while playing stupid, when in reality they fully understand ours. Employers like to hire them for their work ethic. These are the same employers who will complain about the work ethic of American black youths. No matter what one thinks of this problem, the reality is that this is an American problem, and white or black Americans are doing little to solve it. Of course, the politicians hired to solve these problems belong to the first tier of the "I got mine, screw you" philosophy.

50. We'll Explain the Brutality Later, Maybe

Americans rarely dwell on the horrors their history brought to those who suffered our belligerent ways. The Native Americans were defeated and relegated to a life that is worse than that lived by African Americans or even convicts in our prisons. Most Americans know that reservations exist but know less about living conditions on a reservation than they know about atomic physics. And that is OK with everyone—unless, of course, we can sneak a gambling casino onto their lands.

Our democratization of the Philippines is a total failure. Its inability to help its own people in peacetime or in times of national strife is well documented. We actually created the nation of Panama so that we could build a canal. We mentored and dominated them for 70 years or so. Then we went away, leaving only the manuals on how to operate the Panama Canal and their government. Go there and see their poverty, corruption and families living on the earnings of their prostitute daughters.

Never in high school or college did I hear any teacher or professor say that the doctrine of manifest destiny was a horrible thing, or that the era of speaking softly and carrying a big stick was an era of imperialism. I doubt very much that children today are being told anything like the truth about those horrible policies. Hollywood makes movies of our past glories, and small-minded Americans will keep paying the ever-increasing price of the ticket.

51. Accidental Americana

In college, I had a professor by the name of George G. Gnesdiloff for American History. This fellow was an open-minded thinker. Until then, I had always believed everything American and thought that America was as defined in the US Constitution. He made me think, and

I am proud that I met him, but at times, I wish I never had taken any of his classes. It is not a comfortable feeling when most people think I am bad-mouthing America just because I say things that I think are true. If Mr. G. were still alive, he would be a modern version of Diogenes of Sinope, running in the streets shouting the Fourth Amendment to anyone he met:

> The right of the people to be secure in their persons, houses, papers, and effects, against unreasonable searches and seizures, shall not be violated, and no warrants shall issue, but upon probable cause, supported by oath or affirmation, and particularly describing the place to be searched, and the persons or things to be seized.

Almost 50 years after those classes, I see Americans castigating Anthony Snowden for revealing that the NSA has listened to our phone calls and read our e-mails. We now know this, and no Americans have run down the street protesting it. I wonder how hard it would be to convince those self-righteous rednecks—who so sagely prophesize that America will be destroyed by too many Latinos coming here, or by our obesity, or by a hundred other reasons—that the only thing that is killing American democracy is our ignorance and laziness. America's enemy is not in Iraq or any Arab country. The terrorist attacks are but bee stings. The enemy is us, because we are too lazy to learn and do what is right for America, instead of what gets us more money. In 1960 two fellows, Martin and Mitchel, did a similar thing to what Snowden has done lately, and no one screamed bloody murder then, either. A few generations from now the TSA will finger your ass, and the NSA will know how many times you beat your meat, and the only privacy you will have will occur a few days after you are dead, and no one will complain.

52. Another Piggy Bank to Break

Once, long ago, US federal government workers had a retirement plan that had accumulated over $1 billion in invested savings that were going to be used to pay the retirees who had contributed to the plan. There was sufficient money to keep this program going forever, but JFK needed money to make believe that the country was not having financial problems. He took the funds and made that retirement system dependent on yearly money coming to the government. That retirement plan operated without any reserve funds. Government robbery number One went unpunished.

In the mid-1960s, LBJ, the Texas boy who had made good on the Civil Rights front, needed money to make believe that the war in Vietnam did not cost as much as it really was sucking out of Uncle Sam's wallet. Bingo! There goes the savings from the SSAN accounts into the government's general fund, and social security goes on the government pay-as-you-go plan. Social Security was a fund where money that workers contributed went, and whatever was not used was accumulated for future uses. Government robbery number Two went unpunished.

In the 1980s, Reagan and his amateur economists abolished the old government civil service retirement system and put everybody on Social Security, and a government thrift savings plan similar to a 401K was created for government workers. Before long, the billions of dollars that had accumulated in this plan also got robbed, and government robbery number Three went unpunished like the others.

The interesting thing is that if an American company raids its employees' retirement plan, Congress slaps its hands. But when the government steals from the American peoples' retirement plan, no punishment is dealt. It's a sad thing when your leaders not only are incompetent liars, but also rob you as soon as they see your piggy bank. Again, we are the stupid people here, not our leaders. We elect them. Why has the American public not insisted on a training program for these people?

53. Sierra Club vs NRA

In America, there is an organization called the Sierra Club that tries to preserve as much of nature as possible. There is also another organization called the National Rifle Association. It tries to protect the Second Amendment as they understand it, regardless of legal opinions from unassociated jurists. To my way of thinking, the Sierra people are trying to convince Americans that nature has limited resources and that we are wasting them with little regard for the future. The NRA, on the other hand, says that it is OK that 30,000 Americans are shot to death each year. NRA-approved guns don't kill people; people kill people. Can an American mind be less logical than that?

Think of the Sierra Club as a wise, old owl, which instead of sleeping during the day, opts to sit on the edge of the birdbath and teach visiting birds that they can drink the water but should not bathe and defecate in it. The NRA, on the other hand, says, "Hey stupid! It is a birdbath and it is my unalienable right to drink, bathe and defecate in it. And if you don't like it, I am going to bring my gun here tomorrow and defend my right to do it." If the memberships of these respective organizations were to be used as index of American mental ability, there are four times more NRA members than there are Sierra Club members. While the Sierra Club gave you Yosemite National Park, the NRA gives you 30,000 deaths each year. Sad, ain't it? Imagine your generation sporting bumper stickers that say **"NRA: HOW MANY DID YOU KILL TODAY?"**

54. Yes, You are Heroes, but Drop Your Weapons Here

Our soldiers are just like us. Nothing more, nothing less. Some are not trustworthy. That is why our heroic soldiers were disarmed before being allowed in the presence of our fearless leaders when they visited Afghanistan and Iraq. This was a wise move. Why do the generals and the politicians lie to us about these fellows being heroes? If the leaders did not even trust them to have a loaded gun in a combat zone, are they really heroes? Only in America can leaders try to convince adult Americans that laudatory words cannot be so easily nullified by contrary actions.

Let's all grow up and acknowledge that Americans are a strange breed, with good and bad people among us. The bad guys are here, as they are in the military. Look at pictures of Hitler inspecting his Nazis. The troops had bayonets on their rifles. How hard would it have been for one soldier to chamber a round? So, Hitler, the all-time winner of your God's creation of evil on Earth, trusted his soldiers, while our presidents, defense secretaries and senators do not trust our heroes. Blessed be this land of contradictions.

55. Football vs Soccer

In America, there is a feeling that if it something is not American-born or has an Americanized history, it must not be good. Football is an American game, even if it is derived from some other game. It features brutal blows to the body that often disable the opposing players. Retired pro football players move from the arena to the medicine. Since their post-football lives do not interest us, we all think that they just continue on. In reality, most of them have broken bodies when they retire. But when these men are playing, they are superhuman. Their plays are planned by committees and executed by automatons. Whenever an individual player injects ingenuity into a choreographed play, the coach praises him if it brings gains but chastises him when it brings failure.

Football is brutal, and I wish I had been around a few thousand years ago and seen what went on in Rome, for I have a feeling that football, boxing and hockey have more to do with giving the audience joy by watching humans getting beatings than they do with sportsmanship. Then again, I am not yet as American as you, so I may be confused by the ways of the game. I watched my first game on Thanksgiving Day, 1969, with true Americans in Simi Valley, when it was a sprouting redneck heaven and the B-movie actor was still the governor of California. I remember asking a question about why there were no black quarterbacks. Through the years, I have probably watched 100 games because it was an easy way to keep the wife away while I got sauced on beer or wine. For some reason, she tolerated my drinking during football games. Maybe she felt that I was trying to learn to be more American. As I sat there watching those football games, I would often compare them to soccer games:

One so regimented and complex, the other so spontaneous.

One with the possibility of scoring 1, 2, 3 or 6 points and the other with just one point each time the ball crosses the goal line.

One with players protected in gear that makes them look like robots, the other with participants in simple clothing.

Then I would imagine a game between a football team and a soccer team, similar to the types of wars that we fight nowadays:

Gladiators against Christians.

Atomic bombs against a nation that used its aviators and planes to sink US ships.

A B-52 against a sandaled VC.

A tank against a man with an AK-47.

Sometimes I would switch back and forth and stop it all by getting another beer. I did this for years, and finally, when the prince with no brain and his goons went to conquer Afghanistan and Iraq, I came to the conclusion that we would never win any war. It was and would always be a mismatch between our invading warriors and the defending natives. The soccer players would do all they could to overcome the football players, but because of the power of the football players, the soccer players would suffer more casualties. Unknown to the football players and their coaches, the replacement soccer players were right there in the stands. So, while we lost fewer players than they did, they could replenish theirs immediately since soccer is much easier to jump into, participate in, and is more widely played than football. Somehow, American war planners don't seem to understand such a simple thing that I, a nobody, figured out with cold beers. You are mismatched, as you were in Vietnam, and again you lost these undeclared wars.

But there is something about the American character that does stand above it all. When you see a football player down, he has one of two problems. The first is that he suffered a brief pain or dizziness from a hit, and he walks off the field. The second is that he is hurt, and he is carried off the field. Simple and pure, no bullshit Americana. The soccer player behaves differently, however, when tripped. There are three phases to his agony. He shows mortal pain by squirming, wriggling, thrashing and writhing as if someone is cutting his testicles with a rusty knife and no anesthetic. Then he sneaks a peek here and there to ascertain whether the referee has seen him. If the referee is not looking, he goes back to the first phase. When he finally manages to engage the attention of the referee, he gets up and starts playing again. No one takes his acting seriously, and his playing shows no decline. The son of a bitch was faking it.

That is the problem. Americans really do not understand behavior like that in sports or diplomacy or in any aspect of life. This means that we just assume the worst and kill a thousand or a million soccer players. We kill them because we look at life as a regimented football game. We play to win, and if we do not win, we try again. The only variation is that when we lose, we give ourselves a 10- to 20-year time-out before finding some other brown-skinned soccer players to slaughter.

56. Born Ignorant, Raised in Ignorance, and You Get?

Get acquainted with any American redneck, whether an avowed one in the red states or a closet one up North. After having a few beers with the fellow, you will hear that black Americans are inferior at everything, black American women are all on welfare with children from multiple fathers, and black American men are lawbreakers, but God, they are good at sports. If you are dealing with a sophisticated redneck who has read a book or two, you'll hear that African Americans were given all of the help they could get with those giveaways of the 1960s and '70s, and look at them; they still live in the ghetto.

My take on African Americans is that the white American has dehumanized black Americans for hundreds of years. They fought a bloody war to keep them slaves. After the war, it took another one hundred years to get the Civil Rights Act. Then some thinkers figured out that it would require help to assimilate these mistreated humans into society.

The rednecks could never understand that if you mistreat sixteen generations of black people, you certainly cannot give up on them after trying to help them for one or two generations.

So, as a nation, we have a simple problem here. Blacks are Americans, and they are still mistreated. Blacks constitute 14 percent of the population, whereas the American long-term prison population consists of 35 percent black Americans. The problem is simple; find out how to stop putting these Americans in prison or look forward to the day when white America's attitude toward blacks increases the percentage of African Americans in the prison population.

If all of this is not palatable to your dumb mind, perhaps this will help. Newly arrived immigrants will, under the right circumstances, tell you many very bad things about American blacks, just like you do. But wait a minute; you say bad things about immigrants. Think about this. You, as a redneck, believe you are the true American. The American blacks are also Americans. Why not stick together like you did in combat when you needed a white or black man to save your ass? Think about it. You can break rank with ignorance, prejudice and hate, and be the first on your block to have a black family come into your house and share a meal. Do this and it will change your views.

You would be surprised to find out that they are humans, and some are even as dumb and redneck-minded as you are. What if you changed your ways and invited your black coworkers and their families to your house for dinner? What if you found out that they behave just like you and they are as scared as you are the first time you do this? Live next door to a black family and watch your young ones play together, and in their acts you will see the hate that lives in your heart and your black neighbor's heart. And if you are the religious freak you think you are, maybe you would step forward and say, "No, Johnny, we don't use that word," and when Johnny responds, "but you and daddy use it all of the time," then perhaps you can cleanse your heart and show your son some humanity by telling him that it will never happen again. This is much simpler than you think.

57. Guns Save Lives

It seems to me that we don't have the right to live in peace in America because we have let the enemy become us. Those gun-toting children, insane people, and idiots who lose their sanity in moments of hate are defended by the NRA, and we all live in fear. Would the NRA members change their minds if they suffered the loss of one of their own children to gunplay?

The claim that hundreds of thousands of Americans are saved by the simple act of showing a gun during a run-in with thugs is bullshit. Assume that our lawmen kill 500 Americans per year and that the civilian thugs kill about 50 officers per year. So, we have a kill ratio of five civilians to one officer. Not bad. Arm one million Americans and, without the extensive training that is given to the police officers, have these amateurs defend themselves. How many wrongful deaths will there be per year? You have to be stupid to think that guns save lives.

Here is a simpler way for you. The guns in the hands of people made them killers. We hire policemen to protect us from that. Then we allow more guns in the hands of "good" people, and somehow many more in the hands of bad people. The end result is 30,000 dead Americans per year. Our glorious government has accurate numbers on how many policemen die yearly but no data on actual civilians killed by cops. I love it.

58. Another American Oxymoron

The US military has known since World War II that there is a 15 percent or higher fatality rate in combat caused by our own side. Friendly fire is what it is called. Talk about the ultimate oxymoron. There are no bullets that are friendly when they enter your body. If the military, which spends thousands of hours training its people, manages to suffer 15 percent casualties due to its own mistakes, what will everyday gun-ignorant people like you and me cause with guns in our hands? Here is a reality check for you. If you go to the Vietnam War

Memorial, of the 58,000 names written on that cold wall, 8,700 are there because somebody made a mistake. NRA, what if you became sane, and paid attention to reality? Would you still be so obstinate about having Americans suffer so many deaths? And for what?

59. American Christianity, a River without a Current

One of the things that once impressed me about America was that American Christians take Christianity seriously. In Italy, the first Sunday mass was for the mothers and old women. They would go there to pray to God to stop making them pregnant, while the very old would pray to God for a quick death and a release from their poverty and general misery. At the later mass, young women would pretty themselves up and go to church hoping they could snatch a look from a possible suitor so that they could become mothers and old women and go to the early mass. Men and boys would, instead, play cards or billiards in the same bars. In America, Christians go to churches in droves, and that made me believe more Christianity was to be had in America than in Italy. But now that I understand Americans, I know that there are many Christians in America and much worshipping, but there is so little Christianity.

60. When It's Your Time, Go; It Won't Be Better Tomorrow

There is a big problem with the increasing number of older people kept alive by various medical processes. In the past, when an old person became weak and developed a pneumonia, that person would die within a couple of weeks. That was life. Now, we can keep old people alive for long periods of time. Why?

61. Quick Painless Departures

A half century ago, death was a simple thing in Italy. You were alive, and then you were dead. Women would clean your body and dress it. A coffin was either made or bought ready-made. Within hours, you were ready for viewing, and people would kiss the cadaver. I did it, and I still feel weird about it. Within 24 hours, the pallbearers carried you to the cemetery and buried you. Maybe five to fifteen people were involved for only a few hours with helping you transition from life to burial. Getting the death certificate involved a relative going to town and telling the secretary of the commune that someone had died. In America, if you have money, people treat death differently. First, it is rare that you will die at home. You will be in an accident or in a hospital, and these people will be involved with your death: EMS personnel, police, hospital personnel, an undertaker, a coroner, hearse drivers, priests, cemetery workers and whoever else I forgot to mention. In America, even dying is a business.

One more snippet about death. I was four or five years old when I kissed my first cadaver. My mother made me do it. I felt the coldness, and for the next 50 years, I tried to understand why the body felt cold. Eventually, I came across the answer. The body is at room temperature, but your mind knows you are touching a human body, and it expects it to be warm. When it is not as warm as your mind tells you it should be, you conclude that it is cold. It took me over 50 years to figure that out, and I did it before there was a Google.

62. War: a Preventable Disease

Sometimes I wonder how civilization evolved and why I feel like I am really a weirdo when I sense wrong, and everyone else senses normalcy. It is an indisputable fact that old men, not women, start wars. It is also an indisputable fact that young men and women are sent to die in these wars. Why don't those old men go to wars that they start? As the saying goes, in peacetime the sons bury their fathers; in wartime the fathers bury their sons. Should it not be that the sons bury their fathers all of the time?

63. Read the Signs

I have developed the knack of concluding where I am by looking at the lay of the land. A convenience store parking lot with eroded tar where engine oil has leaked means a poor neighborhood. A lamp fastened to the bedside table in a motel means I am in a very shady neighborhood. A restaurant with the cheapest salt and pepper shakers and silverware means that they suffer much theft. A bumpy road, unless you are on I-64 in the Norfolk area, means that it is a poor area, and the city fathers really don't want to invest money in such a place. This one, however, has me stymied: In America, young people and middle-aged people wear clothing with the well-known names of the sellers. They pay more to advertise free for a company. My preliminary conclusion is that Americans are so smart that I still don't understand them, or Americans are so dumb that they pay more to freely advertise for others and don't even know it.

64. Ambassadorship to Japan: $1 Million Should Do It

In America, ambassadorships are meted out as political payback. Ambassadors sent to first-rate countries are from the moneyed class who contributed the most to the political organization that won the presidential election. Ambassadors who are sent to poor, Third World countries are the lesser contributors, or at times, State Department employees who have actual training in the diplomatic areas.

There was an actress by the name of Shirley Temple. When she got out of the movie business, the president made her an ambassador. There is a lady by the name of Caroline Kennedy whose main contribution to society is a sad but classic picture of her and her brother and her mom at the funeral of JFK 50 years ago. She is an ambassador. Rarely is it the case that our ambassadors speak, or read, or write the language of the countries where they represent our interests. The highest American representative to a non-English-speaking nation cannot converse with locals in their own language. Someone said that sending ambassadors that do not speak the local language to a country is like sending soldiers into battles without bullets. How much of this inability to understand the ways of the locals might cause us to start another little war?

65. Opportunity Wrapped in Patriotism

Once upon a time, fear of communism caused America to send a few million American soldiers to Vietnam. Close to 60,000 of these unlucky bastards did not get on the freedom bird that brought the others back to the world. Being that we are what we are, there were people who did not go to Vietnam and instead went Canada, college or got a deferment. I got one of those. Another fellow who got a deferment later became the president behind the curtains, while the prince with no brains was the titular president. Before he became such a patriotic American, that son of a bitch, in the truest and most profane use of the expression, was a draft dodger. When Cheney became eligible for the draft during the Vietnam War, he applied for and received five or more draft deferments. It took him six years to get out of a four-year college. He went to Casper College, which did not even have a football team, and it still took him six years to get out. Of course, he was a good American, and he was arrested for DUI, even back then.

In 1989 *The Washington Post* writer George C. Wilson interviewed Cheney as the next Secretary of Defense; when asked about his deferments, Cheney reportedly said, "I had other priorities in the '60s than military service." Cheney testified during his confirmation hearings in 1989 that he received deferments to finish a college career that lasted six years rather than four, owing to sub-par academic performance and the need to work to pay for his education. Initially, he was not called up because the Selective Service system was only taking older men. Let me explain the logic here. The average age of the GIs that died in Vietnam was 19, yet Dicky was too young to go in? It's magical how things happen in small-town USA.

He applied for four deferments in sequence. He applied for his fifth exemption on January 19, 1966, when his wife was about ten weeks pregnant. He was granted 3-A status, the "hardship" exemption, which excluded men with children or dependent parents. In January 1967, Cheney turned 26 and was no longer eligible for the draft. Why did those true-blue American rednecks who felt that draft dodgers were un-American put that dodger in office and unknowingly make him president, since the prince with no brains from Texas could not do it?

Here is a part that the conservatives don't want to talk about. The war in Iraq was so unwarranted that the only way it can be made logical is that Dicky Boy whispered into the ear of the prince with no brains, "Hey, Mr. President, if you invade Iraq, you can prove to your daddy that you have a bigger dick than he does." It may be crude, but that is the only reason that the son could prove that he was better than daddy. Or was he really stupid enough to think that he had reasons to go to war? Perhaps the liar from Wyoming actually said to the dumb prince, "George, I still have many millions invested in Halliburton; of course, I don't know about that because my wife is managing it and she never, never consults me. If we go to war in Iraq, Halliburton will get a lot of contracts and my investments will increase. Let's go do it and make some money."

Think about there being a God and this God weighing these possibilities:

a. I let Dicky go to war in Vietnam and he gets killed. Sad for his family but good for America.

b. I let Dicky go to war in Vietnam and he, like Oliver North, becomes a war hero. Good for Dicky but bad for America.

c. I let Dicky go to Vietnam and learn about war while being a grunt; upon returning to America, when he becomes the real deal to the pseudo president, the boy prince from Texas, he will talk that poor dummy out of any war.

Had God made the right decision, a or b, America would still have 6,000 live soldiers, tens of thousands of GIs without body parts missing or marred minds, and two to three trillion fewer dollars in deficit. Even though a country's inhabitants are nothing more than collateral damage to our American way of forcing democracy onto everybody, a couple hundred thousand Iraqi civilians would also still be alive. This would have been good for Dicky the Dummy, good for America, and good for the common

Iraqi who knew that he was going to suffer more without Saddam than he suffered with the dictator. And God did miss the boat on that one.

You can come up with your own dream world analysis, but Cheney's absence from Vietnam left America with another stupid man who sends other peoples' sons and daughters to die and isn't even man enough to apologize or blow his impotent brains out when the futility of those deaths are understood even by the dumbest American.

66. People are Always Nice—Look at Our Priest

At times, I am still amazed by how unprepared Americans are for life. I was born in a place where my parents had not read a single book just for the pleasure of reading. Knowledge was transmitted orally, so its veracity depended on how much exaggeration it had undergone as it was transferred from person to person. Yet my parents knew how to feed us and keep us alive without going to the doctor. And they did this under Mussolini's way of doing things, the American way of war, and post-war government, Italian style. We only visited the medical doctor in the town on the rarest occasions. Besides, before the war came to our valley, the doctor put a bullet in the cheek of his wife, and that poor lady still lived with the SOB.

I was born one and one-half years before General Lucius Clay incinerated Tokyo, and then somebody else dropped two nuclear bombs there, and I was born in a place where stupidity reigned. I believed my upbringing was ignorant for many years while living in America. But then an American event occurred that made me feel bad for having had such shameful feelings about my place of birth and my beginning. The event was the discovery that Catholic priests do little boys, as did that famous assistant coach and any number of perverts. When the facts started coming out, and so many Americans showed disbelief that a fellow like a priest would molest a young boy, I finally stopped glorifying America and its ways.

The reason for that was simple. We lived in a valley, and on a nearby mountain there was an abbey known as Monte Cassino. This structure, with its many windows, was like a watchtower over us all. In this abbey, monks and priests turned young boys into monks. Since I was the worst of the litter that mom and dad could have ever made, I was usually punished. The punishment took the form of a sequence of steps. First there were warnings, such as, "If you keep on doing that, I am going to hit you." The penultimate warning went something like this, "If you keep that up, I am going to send you up there," while pointing to the abbey atop Monte Cassino. By the time I was seven years old, I knew that if you were sent up there, the monks would do things to your ass. Young people know many things more than they are credited with, especially in locales where ignorance and religion abound. But telling children the truth about sex and where babies come from are taboos. This is true even though you see roosters mounting chickens, dogs getting locked together, and cows taken to the man who has the bull.

Years later in America, I figured that Americans were truly dumb, for we knew about monks and priests doing little boys so long ago, but in America, many acted surprised when they found the same abuses occurring and the church covering it up. The Roman Catholic Church's management style came from the Romans, and the Romans got theirs from the Greeks, and the Greeks used to believe that a woman's purpose was to bear babies and a boy was for enjoyment. Sometimes, I want to believe that such a simple conclusion about traditions being passed down is just wrong, but sometimes I wonder.

67. If We Were Occupied

I was never in the military, and I was a civilian in Vietnam; therefore, I know next to nothing about war compared to those who fight wars. But I have seen the results of war in Italy and was part of the Vietnam fiasco, so I feel qualified to talk about this. I can tell you with certainty that if war came to America, the following would happen:

    a. Soldiers of the occupying armies would treat you like scum and ogle your women.

    b. The landscape would be scarred, and your house would be rubble.

c. Your fellow citizens, the business-minded ones, would set up whorehouses and other shops catering to the needs of the invaders; for a buck, they would sell their daughters, mothers, honor and country at the earliest opportunity.

d. Your sister would turn to prostitution to feed your mom and dad and everybody else in the clan.

e. You would dream about the freedom that you might have once had, and you would finally understand that humans are greedy and selfish animals despite their intelligence and the hundreds of religions that supposedly keep them from such behavior.

What if the majority of Americans understood that and stopped us from going to war each time we have a new crop of young people? What if our genteel media did show the real ravages of wars?

68. If You Make Nice, It's OK; If You Make Nasty, It's Discrimination

The American concept of freedom has two different faces. When criticism is lobbed at us for the way we treat the Native Americans, black Americans and women, we are ostriches. When others accuse us of being imperialistic, we bomb them, or if we were already bombing them, then we select bigger bombs or new targets. This is where the Americans fail to understand that if you are going to be free, freedom must really be applied to the American minorities and to the citizens of other countries. We really don't understand that our wars of democratization are not a healthy dose of democracy.

69. Vive La France

True Americans, aka conservatives, do not like the French. Just ask any redneck American about the French. Regardless of the fact that he doesn't know how to find France on a globe of the world, he will tell you that the French cannot do this and that. But here is what the French did do:

a.   Their help during the American Revolution was the catalyst that allowed the revolution to succeed. Read about a French fleet and a few thousand French Soldiers in Yorktown and draw your own conclusion as to why the English fellow felt that surrender was a good idea.

b.   The French did not ask us to enter World War I. We entered it because our ships were being sunk, and we always go to war once American business is impeded.

c.   The French did not ask for help in World War II, as the sniveling English did.

d.   The French had 550,000 dead in World War II; the Americans had 418,000.

e.   The French gave America the Statue of Liberty as a gift.

f.   The French abolished slavery in 1795. In America, we fought a war over it and eventually declared all black Americans to be free in 1863, about 68 years after the French. It took us another 100 years to realize we had more work to do. Today, African Americans still have not found that safe American footing so easily found by immigrants.

So, why do rednecks hate the French? Perhaps because some French people are just as stupid as the American redneck and look down at anything that is different?

70. What You are about to Watch Is Very Graphic

When we are bombing other countries and our news networks get videos of the results, our groomed news anchors warn us that what we are about to see is offensive. If you happen to be in the country where the killing occurred, you see pieces of bodies strewn about and people picking up shreds of human flesh. Are Americans too genteel to see the results of our killings? We did the goddamned killing, but we need to shelter our people from it? Bullshit. Show it all; let the taxpayers see if they agree with the way you are spending their tax money.

71. You Make More Money, You Pay a Higher Percentage

American taxation is very discriminatory. No interpretation of the Constitution can ever be made to justify that if you are more talented than Joe Blow, you must pay a higher percentage in federal taxes than Joe does. This is wrong, and it should be changed. America should go to a taxation of a certain percentage, and it should be equal for all—young or old, single or married, seller of religion or seller of deli meats, American overseas or American in America. Stop the preferential treatment and the punitive treatment for those who try harder or are luckier. Everybody pays an equal percentage with no exceptions.

72. Killing Is OK

It seems that the killing of our fellow Americans is a national pastime. There are countries that have per capita murder rates up to ten times higher than ours, but if we can go to the moon and bring the astronauts back alive, sell pecker-enlarging medicine on TV and go to church more often than Italians, how is it possible that Americans kill each other at higher rates than Italians do?

73. God Bless This Dying Soul

In my youth, while still divesting myself of the vestiges of Roman Catholicism, I spent a lot of time thinking about a hypothetical event taking place at the pearly gates in June 1943. Three priests arrive up there at the same time. St. Peter looks at them, and they all have military uniforms on. He points at the first and says, "What did you do on Earth?"

The fellow snaps to attention and says, "I was a preacher in the German Army, and I professed God to my comrades."

St. Peter points to the second, without speaking, and this fellow says, "I was a priest in Mussolini's army, but I did not want to go."

Then St. Peter looks at the last fellow, again without speaking, and the last fellow says, "I was a priest for the American Army, and I gave last rites to hundreds of dying American soldiers."

St. Peter shakes his head and says, "What makes you think that preaching to young men who have killed the men who were preached to by the other priests would get you into heaven?"

I gave up thinking about it because I finally figured out that religion is not the opiate of the masses, but instead, it is the tool used to unify common folk and then send their young asses to die someplace for god or country.

74. She Is Equal Now and She Can Show Her Titties

If you look at a picture of an American commercial office from one hundred or more years ago, you will see more bare skin on the man than the woman in that picture. If you go to an office today, you can look down that slit between the breasts of a woman, and, God, it is still, as it always was, a lovely sight.

But why are women doing that? Are they on the make? Are you showing what you've got because your coworker has less to show? I love it, and I look at it every chance I get, but for a woman to search for equality while showing half of her tits in a workplace will not make her receive equal pay. Isn't it as counterproductive as those black entertainers and common folks that go around saying the N word and expecting no one to call them that? Grow up mentally and achieve with your mind, not your body, and you will achieve equality.

75. Do Like the Others

Long ago, somebody saw the pantaloons the Arabic men wore and concluded that they were better than togas, so we started wearing pantaloons. Eventually, we changed the word to *pantaloni* in Italian and pants in English. Similarly, someone did not like the sheep droppings that were left behind in NYC's Central Park or on the lawn of the White House, and lo, the modern day manicured lawn was born. Our desire to be just like the Joneses has brought us to the point where our lawns have forced us to use too much fertilizer and weed-killing chemicals, and generating pollution from our lawnmowers and other garden tools. We have no qualms with this pollution because we are Americans and we must compete with the Joneses. And this is done for what vain reason? The simple answer is so that we get a greener lawn than the neighbors. This is happening in America; remember the land of the free that you sent poor young bastards to die to maintain? You and I are truly stupid, ain't we now?

76. And the Horoscope Says

I really enjoy people who feel that because they saw a TV program on Nostradamus or a program on the Incan calendar, they know when events will happen. I enjoy them because, to me, it is simply a case of someone demonstrating stupidity without ever being asked. If you ever encounter a man who knows the future, you will most likely find him at a Wall Street trading office or buying just one lottery ticket with his own chosen numbers for each type of game.

Regardless of my opinions about the poor predictors of the future, I think each of us, no matter how stupid or uneducated we are, should have a chance to predict the future. Here is mine. I think that America will someday be destroyed by religions. Here is the way it will happen:

FRIDAY: I cannot work; I am Muslim.
SATURDAY: I cannot work; I am Jewish.
SUNDAY: I cannot work; I am Christian.
MONDAY: I cannot work; I am Moonist.*
TUESDAY: I cannot work; I am a Martian*
THURSDAY: I cannot work; I am a Joveist*

*These new religions will emerge to fill the presently unoccupied days of the week. The names will differ, but the results will be the same.

In case I am wrong with that prediction, then I predict that American political corruption will increase until presidents are picked by corporations. No, that is already happening; see, I am piss-poor at this telling the future stuff.

77. There is engineering, and then there is naval engineering.

The US NAVY is divided in three main branches, The Surface (which is the oldest), Subs and Air.

In the surface Navy, when dealing with actual engineering processes in the engine rooms one has let go of concepts learned in school and adapt to Navy engineering ways. Here is one example:

The Air Navy has airplanes. The airplanes have electronic systems. The electronic systems are wired so that the return side of electrical circuits are attached to the metal of the plane. Same thing happens in your vehicle. The airplanes work just fine.

The Surface Navy does not like that set-up. So they buy ships that have the return side of electrical circuits isolated from the metal of the ships. And the electrical isolation must be maintained. Now think of this: In an engine room there are about 1,000 sensors/actuators that have 2 to 3 wires each. These wires go to terminal connection boxes and then into consoles. If one sensor gets a bit of salt water onto the electrical connection, in few hours the ground isolation is gone. If the ship is at sea, then no one cares. Ah, but if the ship is pierside or undergoing an inspection, then hundreds of hours are wasted finding the pesky wire that got "grounded." Now, if you think about it logically, you will conclude that if the ground is tolerable when underway, then why care about it pierside? Or the other way, assume that the ground is disastrous. Then why are we buying ships that would not work if they suffered a ground during flooding or combat?

But the Air Navy takes a grounded airplane up into the sky and builds high static charges on the skin, hence on the return side, and then when the plane lands on a carrier or on land, the first thing ground crews do is to ground it. And everything electronic keeps on working.

If you have a son or daughter that wants to enlist in the Navy, tell him/her to go into submarine service, or the air, or even better, the US Marines, where everyone knows how to use a gun and a bayonet. Just don't let them get wrapped up into ships with electronic control systems in the engine rooms.

78. Freedom Is Stolen One Itsy Bitsy Bit at a Time

Our submission to speed bumps on public roads is simply a sign of not giving a damn about freedom. If you are not speeding, you should not be punished along with the speeders. Let someone figure out how to implant a bomb up somebody's ass and, Bingo, the TSA people will be putting a finger up your ass, and true patriots will forego the lubricant to save Uncle Sam some money. It is things like speed bumps and passing laws, that are good for you, no matter what shame you have to suffer, that makes Americans think that government is on our side. We should realize that no one has succeeded in violating the Fourth Amendment any better than the government agencies, particularly the NSA, and those other Americans who feel that they are saving the country by obeying the laws. Obeying the law is one thing, but being stripped of your freedoms while doing so is wrong.

79. The US Navy—Truly a Developing Phenomenon

The US Surface Navy has a lot of history, which gives it a lot of tradition, but they are the most mismanaged branch of the US military.

The Navy has almost 250 years of tradition and maybe six months of humanity or progress in treating its people as thinking adults. (I did not originate that, but I have heard that on ships). The surface Navy was the first branch of the military established. It was known as the Department of the Navy and wasn't a branch of the Department of Defense until the middle of last century.

a. During World War II, they had torpedoes that missed the target, and they would fire submarine commanding officers for being poor shooters. Then the cautious COs were fired for being too timid. A year into the war, they finally figured out the problem, and no one went back and apologized to those wrongfully dishonored people.

b. They even bombed an oil slick off of Jacksonville, Florida, multiple times, and each time they reported it as a newly-sunken U-boat.

c. They crucified the skipper of the *Indianapolis*, which delivered the big bomb, and the poor bastard committed suicide. If a presidential pardon was to be used for a good cause, I doubt there would be a better one.

d. They blamed homosexuals for the *USS Iowa* gun turret explosion.

e. They bought the FFG-7 class ships and had to weld bracing bands on their hulls because of cracking.

f. There are more personal and officially-mandated locks on any Navy ship than probably exist in an equally populated US prison or a college dorm, yet the people are all shipmates in the truest meaning of the word. So what if they do not trust each other?

g. The main reduction gears on each ship are locked so that no one, by will or error, puts foreign objects in them.

h. They fired the commanding officer of the USS *Stark* after missiles hit it during the Iran-Iraq War. This happened even though they had Aegis ships in the area, ships that had been sold to American as war platforms that would detect and identify every object in the air and under the water for hundreds of miles around a battle area. That Aegis ship knew nothing, however, about the Iraqi plane that got to the *Stark*. A few years later, the USS *Vincennes*, an Aegis ship, shot down a civilian airline despite its know-everything radars. All of this is public knowledge.

i. The Navy bought the DDG-51 with no helicopter hangers, even though these guided missile destroyers were replacing ships that carried two helos each. After discovering their snafu, they equipped later ships with helo hangars.

j. In the old days, the Navy would throw hand grenades over the side to simulate enemy gunfire, or so I have been told. They had to stop that with the newer ships because the hulls are so thin they would buckle even from the blast of a grenade. No one ties this skimping on thicker steel to the grave damage done to the USS *Roberts*, the USS *Cole* and the USS *Stark*.

k. The Navy has gone to a common access card, CAC, as an ID card. It cost my company $169 to get one for me and three trips to the ID office before it got worked out. This card was to be used in scanners at secure entries, desktop computers and other access points. When they first came out, the gate guard religiously scanned them for about two weeks. Then, the scanning started to become lax. A year later, the guards do not have the scanners any longer. My company spent $169, and the Navy probably paid two to three times more for it. I still need to go through all of the time-wasting routines that I did 30 years ago to board a ship, so why do I have a CAC? One year after getting that CAC, and having gone at least seven months without it ever being scanned, a new policy was enacted. Now we need that CAC and a second picture ID to enter the base. All of that encrypted security stuff did not work, I guess. So we are down to trusting a driver license which costs less than $20.

l. In order to work on Navy ships while in a shipyard, I was sent to a school about safety. The Navy paid for my time. I was issued an OSHA card for this that reads, "10-Hour Maritime: Shipyard Employment." The local shipyard in the Norfolk area, which is organized as a cartel known as the Virginia Ship Repair Association, felt the OSHA-authorized training was not sufficient, so I had to take an online course. This was a somewhat abbreviated version of the OSHA course, for which I had to pay $15 to the local shipyard cartel Of course, I got paid for the time.

m. I have lived a pretty strange life. I was shot at in Vietnam. I have flown in many types of military planes. I have landed and taken off from aircraft carriers. I was even lowered from a hovering helo onto a moving destroyer in the middle of the sea. Three times, I have had guns pointed at my head. One time, I set a record as I went from a full erection to a flaccid appendage when her husband didn't like what he saw. But none of these, or some other un-reportable fearful moments in my life, have ever caused me as much stress as the Navy pass office in Norfolk.

Those ladies in that office, at best a vagabond Navy outpost that deals out regulations depending on the daily mood, make me fear them like nothing else. You stand in line for half an hour or more. When you get to the counter in full compliance with all the posted warnings on your required paperwork, you discover that you do not exist in their paperwork or their computers. There is never a hint that perhaps their paperwork is wrong. They never call their supervisors or decide that I am an American and can go in. Those ladies have achieved the ultimate control. It seems as if they want each male applicant to know that his balls are in their vise. If you are stupid enough to argue with their power, the vise inches closed. When you go back in a day or two after the problem is fixed, they can make you repeat the punishment if they so desire. I concluded long ago that those women sit around at the end of a shift telling stories of how they treated the failures that approached their altar of power. For the suffering I do every time I have to go see those kind ladies, and there have been many different ones through the years, I should be given medals. As in all things in life, there are exceptions. One time, one of the ladies was in a humane mood and, upon telling me that I did not exist in her system, she said, "Oh, I have seen you here before." She gave me the pass.

n. The Navy is always changing, yet literally remaining the same. The modern Navy acts differently; just ask them. Take the way the various groupings of sailors were led in engineering. There was a leading petty officer (LPO), a chief petty officer (CPO), a division officer (DIVO), a Main propulsion assistant (MPA) and a chief engineer. Today, there are a few more layers. The LPO, CPO, DIVO and MPA have the same jobs, but they have added an assistant chief engineer (ACE) and a port engineer. That doesn't count the 10 to 20 tech reps who are aboard the ship almost daily. There are also special teams performing specialized tasks.

When the ship pulls away from the pier for a six-month deployment, the happiest people are the engineers because all of the so-called shore-based assistance disappears. They can schedule their workdays and port liberties without having to worry about us contractor carpetbaggers messing up their day. No matter how disorganized the Navy is, however, there is no other group of people on a ship that works harder or longer than the engineers on a surface ship. These are the people who perform the regular and stupid stuff in the engine and auxiliary rooms. They take apart working equipment and put it back together with procedures that still have errors 10 to 20 years after they were issued. The shipboard engineers must clean the ship because tomorrow some VIP is visiting, or there is a scheduled change of command. They must attend this and that school to make sure they know all the crap that shore-based civilians, people who are really on welfare but think they are working, have passed on to the shipboard sailors. They must study for tests and an ever-increasing list of responsibilities if they want to be advanced. They must be firefighters at a moment's notice. They rarely work fewer than 50 hours each week when things are slow and 70 to 90 hours when preparing for an inspection.

No matter how bright or stupid they are as a group, within each ship there are a minimum of a half-dozen sailors who are eager to work and apply whatever little beads of knowledge have been transferred to them—young people who would do well at anything they tried. These outstanding sailors carry the load, even though the majority of the warm bodies goof off. Sadly, the non-engineering types on the same ship rarely put in a 40-hour week while pierside. To add salt to the wound, they get the same pay and benefits for their respective ranks unless the sailor has dependents and, therefore, earn more money.

So, next time you see a ship go by, try to look beyond the steel plates and imagine hard-working sailors who are unfairly paid for their sweat and do it anyway. There is humanity, patriotism and good will in young people who do as they are told, as their granddaddies and great-great-granddaddies did, while the leadership gets the credit.

80. It's OK to Bomb Them, but Not the Other Way Around

Until the tenth of September 2001, we brought war to other countries without even declaring war on them, and we felt righteous in so doing. The next day, war came to us. During 9/11, I saw nineteen youths bring America to her knees, youths from countries where some still wipe their asses with their hands and then wash their hands in a communal pail of water. I saw that in August 1987 from the window of a hotel in Bahrain and later in Africa and the Middle East. I wonder if anyone else concluded what I did about the 9/11 events. America has been killing and interfering with the Arabic world for years. 9/11 was a payback.

The concept behind the attacks is simple and, unfortunately, nothing new to America, Muslims and the human species. We had the Crusades eight centuries ago, and some Muslims are having their jihads now. The crusaders were promised places in heaven for their families, and the jihadists are promised sex in heaven. The jihadist of today is usually a poor soul who is talked into doing his act, whereas our soldiers are recruited from the unemployed, marginally employed, or hamburger flipping cadre to die in strange lands for fabricated patriotic causes.

Since the 1950s, American foreign policy toward the Arabs has been to check first with Israel to see if they approve. The result is that a nation of less than 15 million people controls American foreign policy in the Arab world. We, the pure Americans who drop bombs from airplanes to give us the distance to forget that these bombs kill humans, feel that if we attack, it is a rational and humane deed. If they attack us, however, they are lowly terrorists. How convenient for the *cafoni* to believe that. That word is Italian. It has a variety of uses that apply to someone who is outright stupid or who engages in contradictory behavior, like an oncologist who smokes two packs of Pall Mall cigarettes daily.

On the day that America was attacked, we had about two million people in military uniforms and probably just as many on what ares known as retainers. Who can count the number of warplanes, helicopters, ships, munitions, cannons and other firearms that we had that day?

We also had five espionage agencies. We had hundreds of thousands of policemen, the FBI, the ATF and border security, and all of these people were too busy building their own little bureaucratic empires instead of doing their jobs. We were spending over $400 billion each year paying these useless defenders and buying equipment that makes the people in the military industrial complex richer. We had more spies than the rest of the world put together. We had embassies all over the world, and each of them had at least one American intelligence officer.

All of these defenders of America failed America, and no one was fired. All of that money failed to defend America. Instead of finding the culpable ones among us and punishing them, the leadership started calling everyone involved heroes, and the propaganda that ensued would have made the Nazis jealous. Even the constitutionally-authorized and NRA-blessed millions of gun-toting last-line-of-defenders-of-America were nowhere to be found that day. There were at least one hundred million guns in the hands of those Americans who will quickly tell you that they are the last line of defense. These are the same Americans who subscribe to the belief that the only way you will take their guns away is to pry them from their dead fingers. Hey, you greatest of all Americans, so lovingly and nobly blessed by the NRA, where were you on 9/11 when America really needed you?

But the real rape of America occurred in the ensuing months, when the mindless and clueless leadership took away basic American freedoms faster than it was done during World War II with the *not-as-good-as-I* Americans. We prostrated ourselves a government that could not govern. Why, the goons and the prince with no brains even gave medals to the guys in charge of the FBI and CIA. They should have been hung in the arched doorways to the buildings where they worked and left there for a few months.

There is always hope in any gathering of stupid people. The American Library Association was the only American outfit with enough courage to keep to its code of ethics and not give in to FBI requests for lists of patrons or the kinds of material they borrowed. When it was necessary to have one American organization that did not kowtow to the panic of the times, the ALA held to its ethics. I am proud of you librarians, as I have always been. As keepers of the knowledge, you stood by your belief s, which come from the ideals of humanity that can be found in thousands of your books Thanks.

81. Some Still Believe Him to be a Hero

I was once much dumber than I am today. I was so impressed by the man saying "I shall return" and "Old soldiers never die" that, at times, those sayings would keep Mac glorified in my head and heart. I even bought and read his book, *Reminiscences*. I really liked the fellow. Then, I accidentally found out that:

He led tanks and infantry down the boulevard where the bonus marchers, former World War I GIs, had built a shanty town.

He rented out the Philippines as a field marshal, the only American General to become a mercenary field marshal.

He left Corregidor even though he had an army superior to that of the Japanese, and Uncle Sam rewarded him with a Congressional Medal of Honor. I believe that is the only time such a high honor has been pinned on such a loser. If you disagree with that, read about the soldiers who were left behind and see what they had to say about it.

He became famous for saying "I shall return." What if he had never left, like the 70,000 soldiers he left behind?

Here are a few other things not said about the American Caesar. When he left the Philippines, he was ordered to leave; he chose a General Wainwright to take over. This general tried his best, but since there was no help coming from America, he had to surrender. Mac got mad. A few months later, General Marshall, the top dog in Washington, put General Wainwright in for a Medal of Honor. Mac, the spoiled brat, nixed it. It wasn't until September 1945 that Truman and General Marshall did put the Medal of Honor on the fighting general.

More on Mac the hero: His famous picture of wading ashore on Leyte was staged three months after the actual event. His island-hopping accreditation was overlooked when it came to skipping the invasion of the Philippines to save thousands of Americans who died in battles that should have never taken place. But the SOB got his victorious Julius Caesar pictures. If you look at the first line of people marching ashore in the picture, there are no Filipinos.

He did a good job turning Japan from a latent believer in their leader as a god into a modern democracy.

He blew it in Korea. Nothing more than a sore loser, he managed to suffer a tremendous retreat. He was fired, and to this day, there are people here who think he was a great general.

82. No, We Are Not as Good as We Could Be

There is a great disconnect in America between freedom and stupidity. A society that allows its children to have children is a sick society. A society that allows its populace to have guns and suffer 30,000 dead Americans from those guns every year is a sick society. A society that sent men to the moon and back over 40 years ago but cannot bring homeless people inside for the winter is a sick society.

If we are to have American-type freedoms and make them work, we must somehow educate people that society, the group of individuals, is more important than individual rights. Keep in mind, however, that if you are being robbed, or drowning or incinerated in a house fire, it is society that comes to your rescue, not freedom. Therefore, stop this crap that it is your right to do this and that because the US Constitution says so; in the end, you need society more than society needs you, and society does not really want to raise your child or pay for the well-being of the survivors of those you killed. This includes, of course, saving drunk rednecks from their burning trailers.

83. American Dishonesty

It is acceptable to steal from Americans, as long as they do not fuss about it. Here is a case of it. American drug manufacturers get tax discounts for investing in research. Grand idea, right? We, the little people, pay more taxes to make up for the money that the drug makers did not pay. Somebody had to pay. Then the company comes up with a new drug, and for seven years they have sole rights to it. Great for spurring inventions. But then those sons of bitches sell us the drug at ten times more than the price they charge the Canadians or the Arabs or anyone else outside the USA. We are the people who made up the taxes that you did not pay. Now, as if we are the dumbest of the dumb, you sell us the drugs we financially helped you make at much higher prices than you sell it for over the border or overseas. You are a crook, and you should be hung by your testicles for two hours every day until you figure out that you are a legalized crook.

84. The Way We Travel Through Life

In the early 1960s, I worked as a dishwasher in the kosher kitchen of a catering place in Queens. The chef, a fat man from Brooklyn who was truly a man of no morals and tried hard to hide his misdeeds, told me that his grandmother had lived her entire life in Brooklyn and had never been outside the borough. For years, I would think about what it would be like to have lived in a town and never left it. Years later, I started noting on long trips that some drivers would follow semis so closely that they weren't able to see the road ahead. I know that you can save fuel if you are in the low pressure area behind a truck, but why miss out on the scenery of the road?

Some people do exactly that with their lives. They are born, become educated in the ways of the adults—which is usually one form or another of not telling the truth—and then choose a trade, a way of life or a religion. They go from birth to death without experiencing the strange and beautiful things that life has to offer. There is much more to living than festering in the compost pile that is life the way it was for your parents. I don't think of myself as anything but a common man, but there are things to do and see in life that require you to lead your own life. Here are a few things that I did or saw that bring back various memories.

One night, on the ship taking us from Italy to America, water came all of the way down to the lowest deck where we were berthed. My mother got scared and sent me to find out what was happening. I climbed all the way to the first open deck and saw that the swinging doors to the bar area had not been locked shot. Waves would hit them and they would open a little and water would find its way down to our berthing area. I thought I had seen fear before, but nothing like that night. I still am very scared of the sea, even though I have gone out on Navy ships 50 or more times in the last 40 years.

I once found a valentine card in my coat pocket from the girl that I loved and thought of as a goddess. She had addressed it "*To Nick*" and accidentally put it in my pocket.

I have been shot at in WWII as an infant and then in Vietnam as a civilian.

After rocket attacks in Vietnam, when the all clear was sounded, I could not stop my knees from involuntarily shaking.

I have dangled from a helicopter while being lowered on a ship that was cruising at eleven knots through the water.

I was making love to a native in a darkened classroom storage closet when a Vietnamese guard opened it, and he shined a flashlight on us and put the gun muzzle against my temple. I do believe I momentarily died of fear.

For a while, I bedded a lady who had the smallest vagina that I have ever encountered and who really liked to tell me about her sex life with other men. She never figured out that I really loved her and was so very jealous.

I have seen grown men cry from fear.

I have seen a Vietnamese father hold his son off the ground with a rope tied to his wrists and passed over the branch of a tree. The son of a bitch was hitting his son's bare legs with a hard stick, and I did not do anything about it.

I have been so stupendously drunk so many times and sensed feelings that I never knew I had.

I have never met an honest man, but I know that he is out there.

Once, on an airplane that was being bounced by turbulence, an older lady asked me to hold her hand because she was afraid. As I did, she talked herself out of her fears, but I thought about how nice it was to help a human being just by holding her hand. That was one of the few times that I had no sexual thoughts while holding the hand of a woman.

Once, during a thunderstorm, I took my young son out on the covered porch and held his hand. I felt the fear in his little hand as each lighting strike illuminated the earth, followed by cracking thunder. I was proud that he did not ask to go back inside. Years later, he thanked me for showing him how to face the unknown and overcome the fear that goes with it.

I walked the circle around Victoria's Peak in Hong Kong in October 1969 and did it again in October 2009. By then, it was called the Peak. I guess the communists did not want to be reminded that they had to sell Hong Kong to the English. Both trips were paid for by Uncle Sam and were not boondoggles set up by me, as is so easy to do when you are using Uncle Sam's money.

I have heard two newly widowed women say the same thing as they sat before their dead husbands: Now that things are good, he went and died. Can you get more selfish than that?

These are a few of the things that I did and saw on my own. I wonder what it would be like to travel from birth to death and only see or learn what other people want you to see or learn or what your little corner of earth offers? Wouldn't it be like driving from the east to the west coast and only seeing the back of a truck?

85. No Jail Time for VIPs

By now, you should have surmised that I really don't know the details of many things. Like the rednecks that I demean, I just do topical thinking and then blab it to death. Right? Perhaps. But think about this. In America, corporations have legal status. How you give rights to an organization is beyond my simple mind, but it has been going on for a long time. If they have a legal right to exist, however, they should also have a legal right to be punished. Here is how the tobacco industry handled a situation in which it was taken to court, and the tobacco corporations walked without being punished.

For decades, those good tobacco-packaging Americans were spiking the tobacco so that smokers would have a stronger addiction than if they had smoked untreated tobacco. After years of legal wrangling, those

corporations made a deal with the government: OK, we will pay billions
of dollars to this and that, but we are not going to admit any wrongdoing. The government lawyers, the ones who could not get jobs with the
big renowned firms, patted themselves on the back, and everyone was
happy. The bastards at the tobacco companies had decided prior to the
agreement that they were going to raise the price of tobacco products.

So, in the end, today's smoker is being screwed twice. First, every
state agency that can add some taxation to a pack of cigarettes does so.
They do this with a righteous sense that if smoking is bad for people, why
not punish the smokers by making them pay more. No, addiction to nicotine is not a recognized medical issue; now if you do heavy drugs, come
on in, and we will help you. Second, the tobacco companies are making
smokers pay those billions of dollars that the companies, who are legal
entities, promised to pay. Why were the wrong people punished?

86. American Pedigree

Non-pedigreed families in America can ascend the social ladder
in various ways. The pedigreed could be defined as the Rockefellers,
DuPonts, Vanderbilts, Astors, and hundreds of other old-money families. To reach these stratospheric ways of living, you need to accomplish something. Gates and Buffet are there, but it will take a couple of
generations for the money to be properly transformed into the pedigree warranted by the rich.

There are also people who have qualified by becoming known to
society, and as soon as they get their billions, they too will be allowed to
ascend into pedigree-dom. Here is how it works. Grant, Ike, McCain,
Dole, Inouye, and others got to the first rung of the pedigreed level
by using the military. Others used the political system. In the state of
New York, the established path to a pedigree is by becoming a city or
state attorney general. Ask the Cuomos, Giulianis, and other wanna-be
or soon-to-be pedigreed Americans. Ah, but you and I don't have to
worry about such status. A thousand years ago, our forefathers were
peons, and now we are free men in a land of the free. We can pay taxes,
use the benefits of that taxation, and even feel proud, but pedigreed

we will never be. Have we really changed from the status of our forefathers one thousand or two thousand years ago?

87. The Ultimate and True God

America has, by design or accident, managed to create the ultimate religion acceptable to all. That religion is simply the almighty US dollar. The idea of immigrants coming to America for freedom occurs rather infrequently, and it did exist in big proportions when the European Jews figured out that Hitler was not a nice guy. But the millions and millions of people who have come here through the centuries and now sneak over the border are here because we have the ultimate god, the dollar.

Here is how this religion works. You come here and you work and you get paid. You work two jobs, and you get paid accordingly. You work overtime, and you get more money. You show up on time, do your work diligently and produce more than your coworkers, and you will be the last one to be laid off unless, of course, the company gets sold. This is the real reason immigrants come here. It is a religion to them because it's the only promise that is usually kept. Their homespun religions promise them happiness only after you die. America gives you happiness after so many hours of work. That is good.

Please don't tell those who follow that America offers freedom and all that malarkey; America offers you a good living if you want it. And that, believe it or not, is more than many other countries will ever do for their people. Few of the people that come to America and stay ever give up on their country of birth. There is always an emotional obligation. In reality, that is truly idiocy. Look fool, your country is like your mom. If your mom lets you go because she cannot feed you, then you really have no obligation to your mom. It is that simple.

88. Once Upon a Time, Chad

The distribution of knowledge in America seems to be based on convenience. Take the case of polling machines. How is it that states cannot get foolproof voting machines so that accurate counts can be made on the first pass? Let's go back to the stolen presidency. Do you remember? Here was a state that has had a space program for over 50 years, yet it cannot buy a machine that punches through a voting ballot. Thus, America was introduced to chads. Remember? In the 1970s, while I was working as a computer programmer for the city of Los Angeles, we used IBM card punches, and we never had a problem with Cchads. The technology to cleanly punch a card was there a long time ago. But 30 years later, Florida invented a new way to screw America with its chad. Read about the web that Katherine Harris wove.

89. No, it Is Not $3.50/Gallon, it Is $3.499/Gallon

America, the land of no nonsense, is so dumb at times that we are led to believe that if we buy something for $3.95, we are not really paying $4.00. Or even dumber, why do they waste money and materials marking fuel prices for, say $2.99 and 9/10 cents? Think how much time and calculating effort would be saved if we were told that the fuel was $3.00 per gallon?

90. Making the Inspector General Office Immune to Local Yokels

The inspectors general are presently part of the same organization that they are to inspect. Since their performance (i.e., promotions) depends on the local supervision, the process is about as sane as putting the fox in charge of watching the chickens. What if the inspectors general worked for the Office of Management and Budget? In the end, the wrongdoing that these inspectors look at is of a financial nature, so they should work for the people that run the accounting. It certainly would free them from local command politics.

91. We Got the Money, We Make the Pollution

Once upon a time, Los Angeles had a fairly efficient transportation system. Then, some companies decided to buy it. Here is what

Wikipedia has to say about it: "The General Motors streetcar conspiracy (also known as the Great American streetcar scandal) refers to allegations and convictions in relation to a program by General Motors (GM) and other companies who purchased and then dismantled streetcar and electric train systems in many American cities." Between 1936 and 1950, National City Lines and Pacific City Lines—with investments from GM, Firestone Tire, Standard Oil of California, Phillips Petroleum, Mack Trucks and the Federal Engineering Corporation—bought over 100 electric surface-traction systems in 45 cities including Baltimore, Newark, Los Angeles, New York City, Oakland and San Diego and converted them into bus operation. Several of the companies involved were convicted in 1949 of conspiracy to monopolize interstate commerce but were acquitted of conspiring to monopolize the ownership of these companies. Somewhere, descendants of the heads of these companies are enjoying the money they made at such a cost to nature. I bet they are the first to bitch about smog. If there were a God, would you not think that he would punish someone for this?

92. Cheap Printers, Expensive Inks

Am I the only dummy who thinks that it should be illegal for a company to sell you a printer for less than $150 but then charge $50 for each cartridge of ink?

93. A Smart President? Are You Kidding?

The American way of electing officials to high offices often results in people of little ability filling seats of great responsibility. Take the case of a then-unknown man called Trent Lott. The boy is truly an idiot from Pascagoula, MS. He went to Washington as a politician, and after having amassed sufficient political stock, he was chosen to be the senate majority whip. This happened in the era of President Nancy Reagan and the movie actor who thought he was on camera in the Oval Office for his entire eight years there. Trent was a dumb boy. But that did not influence his rise to the senate majority whip. Now ask yourself, was he the only idiot to get there, or are there other states that send their incompetent sons to wreak havoc in Washington?

94. Where the Dummies Lived

In 1974–75 I resided in Pascagoula, MS, living off taxpayers' money while working on a US Navy project. Thank you. By then, I had already lived in three different countries for over a year each and had also lived in three different American states for a year or more each. What I saw in Pascagoula was strange. When the local shipyard, the biggest employer in Mississippi and Alabama, would pay its people, some of them would run to the grocery store, buy beer and ice, pull folding chairs off their pickup trucks and start drinking beer in a shady area of the parking lot.

On one side of the city, there was a factory that turned fish into fertilizer. On the other side, there was a paper mill. In August, coming out of the apartment would cause you to first try to hold your breath until you couldn't anymore and then make you want to puke. The natives did not mind it since it was employment.

On the first sea trial of the *USS Spruance* (DD-963) in April 1975, while in line to get lunch, a shipyard worker took his helmet off, and without even removing the liner put three scoops of chicken a la king (a classic of those days) into the safety helmet. This happened even though the slob already had heaping mounds of food on the serving tray.

While fishing on Saturday morning, a local tried to convince me that stealing pencils and small items from your employer was OK, but stealing high-cost items made you dishonest. Some Americans are so stupid as to think that honesty is a graduated value that can come in quantities, such as a little, some, half and full. In Pascagoula, I found a local who explained it all to me.

There were many other incidents to point out why Pascagoula, MS, was the bottom of the American abyss of ignorance, but I would get in trouble for telling.

95. The Right Way, the Legal Way, the Navy Way

The Navy again. There are simple guidelines in life that help those who try to be honest, but most people get caught in the eddy of times and either rationalize their wrongful ways or, if lucky, never realize the evil of their ways. In the US Navy, there are so many money-wasting programs that create dishonorable people. It happens simply because people make decisions that waste millions of taxpayers' dollars, decisions they would never consent to if it involved their own money. This is dishonesty.

If this claim doesn't seem worrisome to you, read the history of the first in a series of ships called the *USS San Antonio* LPD-17. Even the dumbest American would have never wasted his or her money that way. People should have gone to jail or exiled to countries where *they still make canoes out of trees.*

96. When I Moved Here, There Were Fields

In the fall of 1964, a classmate and I rented a room from a Mrs. Allen in Inglewood, CA. She lived close to the intersection of Century and LaBrea. She was an older widow who would often talk about her husband, who was gassed in World War I, and some hotel where she worked. She would often say that when she and her husband had moved to Inglewood, it was just a grouping of a few houses here and there with large bean fields south of Century Boulevard. Now it had become a "conurbation." I asked her about the word, she spelled it for me, and I learned its meaning.

I wanted to like her and have her like me because she was the first American woman that knew nothing about Italians and was not from NYC. To me, she was truly American. But the lady did not like me. I just felt it, and later I would classify her as the first true xenophobic American that I had met. To this day, however, whenever I fly at night anyplace over this earth, I can see the conurbation she was talking about, signaled by the endless bright lights of cities and sparse patches of darkness in between.

97. Generals, Incompetent or Dishonest

American generals and admirals know whether a war can be won or lost before they start the fighting. Therefore, if our side did not know whether Vietnam, the first and second Iraq wars and Afghanistan could not be won before they started them, we have piss-poor generals and admirals. Knowing that the war cannot be won, American generals and admirals send other people's children to die. Is this honorable?

98. Let's Us Denigrate Them Foreigners

American movies sell American ways to foreign nations. American movies about Mexicans and all other Central and South Americans depict the locals as outright idiots. They are made to play stupid and demeaning parts. Chickens and pigs on airplanes and other demeaning and xenophobic clichés are always part of American movies that deal with those who dwell south of us. Why? Are we really that superior to all others? No. It is simple stupidity. Other countries, such as France, England, Italy and Germany, do not make films demeaning Americans. Imagine Switzerland making a movie about love, American style, with a drive-by shooting in the opening scene. We are not smarter or better than other citizens of this Earth; we just go out of our way to show our ignorance and insensitivity.

99. Hate is as American as Americans

You have to understand hate to understand the way we treat legal and illegal Latinos. We do not have American citizens who want to pick vegetables, wash commodes, work as ditch diggers and perform other dirty low-paying jobs. The Latinos face hardships created by their corrupt governments and the Roman Catholic Church. Here, they strive to make a marginal living and send money home to their relatives. They come here to survive and be useful humans, legally or illegally, and we treat them as dirt. These poor sons of bitches, who, unlike us, do not know where their next meals are coming from, do those things that the Americans do not want to do. Bingo. The American idiots, rednecks, liberals and all other overt and closet xenophobic bastards have bad things to say about these poor people. The same bastards who do this feel that every visit to their place of worship will cleanse their hearts of hate. Bullshit; you are mean people, and if you ever have to search for work so that you can eat, then perhaps you will understand. One or 20 generations ago, your ancestors were treated the same.

100. Susie, Let's Celebrate That I No Longer Molest You

I know I harped on this before, but it is not senility that makes me revisit it. I really do not understand why we set aside time to celebrate the wrongs we have done to parts of American society. Things like appreciation months and days—for example, Black History Month or Hispanic Heritage Month or Women's History Month—are, to me, really sad. Imagine a father who has been raping his daughter for a long time, then stops and forces his daughter to celebrate the anniversary of the day he stopped raping her. How sick are we? What was done and is still being done to black Americans, Hispanics and women are the evil ways of a society that, though it escaped European tyranny, has managed to set up the same abusive processes here in America. If you want to celebrate the ways of other people, give them opportunity, equality and civility, and everything else will work itself out.

101. So They Like Men Taller Than They Are

The next time you are walking down a crowded street, look at all of the couples. You will soon notice that the women are usually shorter than the men. This is an oversight on the part of women who want all to know that they are just like men but fail to break the animalistic need for protection by men who are taller than they are. If you are going to be equal, don't stoop to tradition; be equal. I wish I would be around for another 50 years to see if homosexual couples adopt the same height differential crap. It's OK if I miss it, though.

102. Plastic Flowers

A long time ago, I took my mother to the cemetery to pay respect to my dead father. While climbing the steps of the mausoleum, she looked at the fields of headstones with plastic flowers and said, *Chisti Americani so pazzi, mettene gli fiuri di plastico su gli sepulcri.* "These Americans are crazy; they put plastic flowers on the graves." You would never give your mother or loved one a plastic bouquet. Yet on a grave, you accede to the wishes of the lazy cemetery workers and you give plastic flowers to those whose memories you are trying to honor.

I believe that your inability to stand up to a groundskeeper in the cemetery makes you a total wimp. These little agreements you make with the world without paying attention to the values that you cast away make you part of a warring country, and you don't even give a shit that your tax money is killing others. When the news anchor says that American planes bombed such and such, do you have any sensation that we just killed some people somewhere, and you and I were responsible for it? Do you find it hypocritical that you live by a rule that says "thou shalt not kill," yet you go right along with capital punishment? My mother was the most uneducated person by the American standards of her times, but she was a hell of lot smarter than most Americans that I have known because she was able to call it as she saw it.

103. Americans May Be Belligerent, but They Are Fearful, Too

When it comes to human behavior, the hardest thing to discern is who is really smart. Take the case of bin Laden. The wanna-be engineer was involved with heavy attacks, and in a sense, he succeeded. But my technical sentiments say that he failed to actually achieve his goals. The airplanes hitting the World Trade Center buildings were supposed to make the buildings tip over and fall in opposite directions and cause much more destruction on the ground then they did. In the end, he failed.

He was a stupid, uneducated man who understood the ways of camels more than he understood American building codes. Ah, but then everybody gets lucky at least once in his life. He never even considered the effect of his plans. During the last decade, because of the 9/11 attacks, trillions of dollars have been lost, freedoms have been lost and Americans walk around scared. He never planned for that. He never knew what would happen. But somehow Americans reacted this way because of the novelty of the attack, or the fact that it could take place, or from the realization that we are a country whose diplomacy consists of sending B-52s to drop bombs when we do not get our way. So, was he a smart man or a dumb shit like the rest of us?

104. Elsie Does Not Need DST

Daylight Saving Time is a waste of money. The cows get up at sunrise, the rooster crows on his own time, and we have electrical lights that illuminate the night as if it were day. Why play the game of changing the time twice per year and cause problems? There are sections of Americans that were smarter and never have done the silly time-changing thing.

105. Why do Americans Get Hooked on the Bermuda Triangle and Other Stupid Superstitions?

Why has no one bothered to explain to people who believe in the Bermuda Triangle that there are many more cases of airplanes having crashed on mainland America and never found than anywhere else in the world? What is the BS about Bigfoot and the Loch Ness thing? I seem to remember that people who created those stunts have come forth, or am I losing it?

106. Testicles, Beaks and Anus, AKA American Cold Cuts.

Why don't we care what kind of meat is in our expensive cold cuts? When I first came to America, I worked in a grocery store. I started out at $15 per week, working three hours after school and twelve hours on Saturday. The store would get freshly cooked hams, roast beef and turkey breasts. These would be cut and sold as cold cuts.

Not too long ago, I was in a very chic grocery store in Williamsburg, VA, a store that serves the gated communities surrounding it. I asked for unprocessed meat, either beef, ham or whatever they had. They had no such thing. I explained to the wannabe butcher that what he was selling was processed meat, and he looked confused. Does anyone know what is in those chunks of processed meat that are chemically made to taste as if they were the real thing? Does anyone care, or is going to be shocked to discover someday that those meats came from cow anus?

Or is going to be like the shock you suffered when you discovered what the priests did with young boys?

107. American Tanks and Russian Tanks

In college, we had one of those reborn Christian teachers. Mr. Dillon would try to explain science with religion. One day in spring 1965, he told me that soon American tanks would fight Russian tanks on the hills of Palestine. I asked him where he found that information, and he told me it was in the Bible. I rode my bicycle to the Christian store and bought a Bible. The next Monday morning, after having read the entire thing during the weekend, I told him I had found no such thing in the Bible. The son of a bitch had the gall to tell me that it was all in the interpretation. I never read the Bible again or listened to the interpreters of such writing. I guess when Israel invaded Palestine, Mr. Dillon went around saying, "I told you so."

108. We Decrease the Product but Keep the Price

In 1971 I was making soup and had run out of Lipton onion soup packets. I walked to the store and bought a box of it for 33 cents. I went home, and inside the box there were only two packets instead of the three packets that had always been in the box. The outside of the box said so, but the darn thing cost the same as if it had three packets. It was a 33 percent reduction in product for the same price with no announcement to the unwary, or a magical 33% rise in price without telling the buyer. That was the first time I experienced what has become a normal and daily shorting of contents that the manufacturers just happen not to tell us about. What if we, the users, stopped using these products as soon as the manufacturer pulled such a stunt?

109. We Are the Junkiest of Them All

I really do not understand why, in every city in America, people need to rent storage units. Don't they know that what they have is just too much junk, and they should part with it before its value becomes less and less after they figure in the rental fees?

110. MIC at Work

The American military industrial complex has been copying German World War II equipment and not even saying thank you. The present American helmet is very similar to what the Germans wore in World War I and World War II; it is most likely not as durable or protective, but it looks the same. During World War II, Americans copied the German fuel container, which the English had derisively named the Gerry Can. The telephone wire was also a copy of the German telephone wire. Bell Labs did that. The jet engines and the jet planes were first made in Germany. The modern American M60 machine gun is a copy of the German World War II MG42. Why do we need so many engineers and scientists in the military industrial complex when we are copying from others?

111. Let's Zap the Liar

Are Americans better humans than citizens of other countries? In 1965 my college professor, Mr. Gnesdiloff, introduced our philosophy class to the Stanley Milgram experiment, which had taken place in 1963. The experiment involved having people push buttons that supposedly resulted in electric shock to unseen individuals when they failed to provide the desired answers to posed questions. The results were cataloged according to degrees of pain given to the man behind the curtain, who was actually just a tape recorder. Eighty-one percent of the participants pushed at least one button and gave an electrical shock to a make-believe human. In time, the experiment was repeated in other countries and the 81 percent rate was duplicated in each country. The moral of the story is that Americans are just humans. We claim to be superior to others, and some of the others think of us as superior because we can go over and bomb anybody and get away with it. When we are not bombing somebody, we are discriminating against each other or killing each other. But America is superior to all other nations because we have the ultimate religion, the almighty dollar.

How to Change America

Until now, I have ranted and raved about all that is wrong with America. Now, I would like to propose some ideas on what to change and how to accomplish it. Remember that these are the ideas of only one person, a person who thinks strangely. There is a very good chance that other people out there have better ideas. No matter whose ideas you go with, however, try to understand that we need change in America, and we must do so without any harm coming to anyone. This is what I recommend. Take it or leave it.

1. Elect Women into Any and All Offices

This should be the first goal for future Americans. Electing women into leadership is an urgent fix to the travesty that this Earth is suffering. We have been led by religious men, by make-believe religious men, by educated men and by idiots, and to this day, we still kill, hate, prey on the poor and treat women as a subspecies, unwittingly destroy our motel room, and brag that we are superior to all other species. If women are elected into office in numbers proportionate to the population's ratio of women to men, we would be better off. No matter what political affiliation you have, campaign for women. Elect women. Here is why:

a. Men have been in charge since the beginning, and look at what we have.

b. Men evolved as the hunters, and inseminators, and possibly as protectors. This mentality has made them belligerent, chancy and outright stupid in some cases. Throughout history, our male leaders have followed the ways of their fathers and either blocked progress or made things worse.

c. Women have a greater investment in the making of humans than men. It is doubtful that women will so easily send their sons and daughters to die in wars or continue allowing them to be gunned down on the streets.

So give women a chance. It may be the last chance you have. If women leaders turn out to be just as poor at leading humanity as men, what hope have we then? Computers?

2. Religion and Government: Splitting the unhappy couple

Religion and government do not mix. America started out that way, but it was intended to have a Christian government with lip service given to the separation of church and state. The Christian believers, being of slow wit, have forced their religion upon the government. In case you do not agree, think about this:

a. Sunday is a Christian holiday, not Jewish, not Muslim, not atheistic or agnostic. It is Christian.
b. Using the Bible to mark the taking of office of high-ranked politicians is Christianity at work. The Jews, agnostics, atheists and Muslims do not use the Bible.
c. Having stores closed on Sunday and not working on Sunday arose from the blue laws.

Claiming that we have separation of church and state is like going down the street convincing others that your natural mother, who had sex with your natural father and gave you normal birth through the birth canal, is still a virgin. Separation of church and state must be made complete so that the religious do their things and do it without even causing a traffic problem at the church on Sundays for the non-believers. Religion creeping into the government can be attributed to the ignorant few Americans who have found God and want to smother all others with their findings.

3. In God We May Not Trust

Putting "In God We Trust" on money is a religious statement supporting the Judeo-Christian God—not Buddha or Lucifer. The phrase was added by Congress after an idea was put forth by a Reverend M. R. Watkinson, or so the story goes. Is every American worshipping that same single god? Can you imagine a Muslim or Buddhist US president? If not, then Judeo-Christian faith is not the religion of America, even if we were supposed to have religions in government. Give to Christ, Mohammed, and God whatever you want as an individual, but do not involve the government.

4. Wake up to American Reality

In America, we are truly out of touch with reality.

    a. An American woman spends hours making herself beautiful and bares half her breasts at work, yet she expects to be treated as a human instead of a sex object. If this is what women want, the only way to get equality is to castrate virile men.

    b. Politicians lie to us, and we do nothing about it.

c. We expect politicians, priests and other authority figures to be more moral than we are. We complain when they turn out to be like us.

d. We blindly spread rumors. There may have been spitting on Vietnam veterans in the San Francisco airport, as claimed by some. How can one disprove that? But the Nixon people and movies like *Rambo* and *Hamburger Hill,* it was stated as a fact. So now it has become fact to those who wish it so.

e. An American man spends less time thinking about the way he is treated in America than a dog spends searching for a satisfactory place to crap. Yet an American man will advocate the injection of religion into government, proliferation of guns and undeclared wars with countries that are populated with brown people.

5. Demystify our Leaders

In the beginning, we gathered in caves, and the man with the biggest club told us what to do and what not to do, if we wanted to stay in his cave. A few millennia later, we gather in so-called nations, where people with the most money or ability to get other people to give them money or allegiance become cave governors, and they tell us what to do.

The way we pick leaders, or the way leaders are forced upon us, is not as important as the simple fact that our leaders are mostly useless, egotistical maniacs who love power. We, the peons, are dumb enough to deify these morons, and the end results are always the same. They own the cave, and they can send some of us to war, increase our taxes or change the rules so to achieve their own goals. We are then told that we elected exactly what we wanted.

We pick our leaders similar to the TV show on which you are given the choice of Door Number One or Door Number Two. But the deal is rigged. Some moneyed people have given us only the two possibilities, and we can only pick Door One or Door Two, even though most people know that neither One nor Two is capable of earning an honest day's wage.

Here is how we could train leaders. Change the objective of the US Naval Academy from its present military form to a national leadership academy. Applicants who want to be leaders and have a B or better grade point average in high school would be randomly selected to enter it. The training program would include foreign languages, diplomacy, leadership and basic human rights.

The leadership academy could develop training programs for developing nations or nations that have failed to develop. The student would be required to live overseas with poor natives for a minimum of one year. The students, upon graduation, would work with city, state and federal agencies to earn a higher degree. With this higher degree, the graduates would be qualified to run for local positions, such as city council person or mayors, or they would be qualified to enter the Foreign Service. Above all, we should teach these people wisdom.

Ten percent of the entering student body of the national leadership academy would be foreign students. The academy would select these students using the same random process, rather than taking the children of dictators or other usurpers of power. This new institution would also do research studies on the needs of emerging nations, the best ways to allow people to achieve autonomy, how to get Israel out of Palestine, how to get peace in Ireland, how to get poor Americans out of the ghettos and barrios, and, of course, how get the Native Americans out of the prisons that we call reservations. If thinkers are allowed to guide us through peaceful pathways, so that all humans live without the horrors of wars and poverty, it will be a better Earth.

The reason I picked the US Naval Academy to become a leadership school is because of its start. Its roots come out of Somers Mutiny, the last hanging on a Navy ship, and I don't believe they ever developed the leadership core that was dreamed of in 1845, so why not abolish it and give it a second chance by reopening it as a leadership school?

6. Change the Educational System

Whatever teaching schemes were developed a couple of centuries ago are still in use despite the fact that not all humans learn the same way. The first 10 to 14 years of schooling should be seen as nothing short of children entering an educational factory and coming out as useful citizens at the other end. This would replace the present process, in which high school graduates are mostly uneducated youths who wasted twelve years in school systems whose main product was anything but educating children. Imagine an eighteen- to nineteen-year-old American being able to logically separate facts from the fiction that spouts from the mouths of politicians. Imagine future generations of Americans who can separate facts from bullshit and elect leaders that remain committed to their goals.

To develop a better and reality-oriented training system, re-vamp the United States Air Force Academy as an experimental university on education. Have student bodies selected on a random basis, and train teachers who can instruct on subjects presently taught but also direct students on how to live within society. No religion, no morals; just the laws and the fact that each human has a right to live without the fear of the bullies or the police or the rich people. The concept of making a diligent, law-abiding, and productive citizen after 13 years of schooling is achieved on a random basis by our current system. It should be a guaranteed process.

How hard is it to see that Americans, like the rest of people in the world, really do not know how to teach honesty, religious and political tolerance and race and gender equality?

Train the educators and let them educate, and if mommy and daddy feel superior to the system, then enroll them in a communist-style re-education camp. Get the syllabus for this camp from North Korea. The present system of allowing anyone to raise a child as they see fit until the child becomes an adult criminal and burden on society is not right.

I am a product of international schooling that did not work. I was educated in post-war Italian schools. It was common there for teachers to slap children on the face and back of the head, or hit them with open hands or with a wooden stick. I was a failure in school. I repeated grades. I failed out of one college in America. Though I could get top grades sometimes, I never discovered how to study, or how to take tests, or how to be the average student. By the way, during seven years of schooling in Italy, I never heard a teacher say anything about Mussolini, neither was there anything written in books about the fellow. It's neat how people forget their snafus.

The older I get, the more I think that perhaps schools are not really able to deal with a child with any mental functions that differ from their model student. In America today, millions of youth are processed through schools and sent out to the world with little ability to compete. The fast food restaurants have cash registers that have pictures of the product, and the machine puts out the correct change. This is not progress; this is science rescuing us from our scholastic ineptitude. The current methods of schooling were archaic when I was young and most likely are worse today.

7. Shake Up Our Un-heroic Military

We have wasted trillions of dollars and killed millions of people by obeying the will of the military industrial complex. If the world is a better place than it was 100 ago, it certainly isn't due to war. Here is what could be done with the US military:

Change from the four-branch military to one unified military. The present structure is inefficient and causes the military to have nearly a thousand general officers, yet no ability to win wars.

Use the graduates of the United States Military Academy, West Point, to enter service with all of the military. The ground forces would be trained like the US Marines or US Army Airborne. Aviators and support personnel would be trained the same way, with specialization, such as land- and sea-based aircraft, after their basic training.

We have too many military leaders costing too much money. Instead, pay the experts their open market value, including cost-of-living increases, as long as they remain experts and keep doing the same work. Promote people who genuinely want to lead, are qualified to lead and will excel. But make it so that promotion is not the only way to earn a good salary in the military.

Above all else, go back to the draft. Sons and daughters of congressmen should get to go die in another folly to export American democracy to countries where they still wipe their asses with their hands. Get everyone to go instead of luring poor youths with pay and benefits that are far superior to those available to them working in the few remaining factories or flipping hamburgers. The higher pay and honorific status presently given to anyone wearing a uniform does not change the simple fact that America has a mercenary military. Because it is a mercenary military, it can be dispatched without any fear of rebellion from within the ranks. Reactivate the draft, and get everyone to serve their country; whether the service is to mentor poor kids, clean the streets of ghettoes, work in old people's homes, replant trees in burned forests or serve in the military. Everyone should give some time to the nation.

Before any soldier is sent into battle, he or she should be made to read books like *All Quiet on the Western Front, Slaughterhouse Five, The Red Badge of Courage* and similar personal books on war. Any soldier who is about to kill should know what soldiers before him felt. They should be made to think about their mothers' worries and picture the same circumstances for the mother of the enemy soldiers.

Before soldiers go into combat, we should let them choose what they wish on their tombstones. Obey the freedom of speech and honor the wishes of a dead soldier who chose an epitaph, "America, why the fuck did you kill me?"

Get rid of special privileges for military personnel, such as shopping without paying sales tax, military discounts and not paying tax on all earned income, such as special pay for combat duty, extra pay while at sea or living quarters allowances. Enlisted men have always looked at their military stints as a job. The glorification and benefits come from rotten old people like you and me who send these youths to die.

Here are some other things that can be done with the military to stop the waste of money:

a. Get rid of the base exchanges. Get Walmart or another retailer to run these stores and charge taxes on all products.

b. Get rid of the expensive and laborious processes of changes of command. The lower-ranked military personnel spend thousands of hours dressing up the bases and ships and their uniforms so that some general can have another shiny moment in the sun. In reality, the military does immediate changes of command when it fires a commander for cause. That process takes a few minutes and costs very little money.

c. Stop the US Navy from buying equipment that they do not know how to operate and maintain. This causes cavalcades of civilians to help them out, at a price. Either decrease the complexity of equipment, or assign trained, degreed engineers to be part of a ship's force.

9. A Couple Ideas on Quelling Our Appetite for War

To eliminate our gusto for wars, change the mechanism that gives us wars. Elders start wars and send the young to die. Let's change to the following:

All countries raising an army must establish the minimum age of conscripts as 60 years of age or older. Just imagine a meeting of the president or prime minister and his advisors to talk about going to war, and then telling an 80-year-old army general to go die someplace. Forget it. Even if the general is willing, he could never convince his hemorrhoid-laden army to go fight. I know your first reaction is to think of this as utterly stupid, but what is logical about sending the young to die in wars that the old have started? Somebody has to make older people understand that once they enjoyed the benefits of their country, they are obliged to defend it for those that come after them. At present, the young die, and the old enjoy life and become parasites on society with the medical needs of old age.

Another possibility is to change the Geneva Convention to include execution of leaders of the warring countries and their immediate families. First, we would publicly execute the leaders in the countries that started the war, and then we could execute the leaders and their family in the countries that defended themselves. Think what this would do for peace. Also note that in the old times, the families of the losers in wars did not fare well, so we are not going into new territories here. If a US president takes it upon himself or herself to send the child of an ordinary citizen to die in war, what is fairer than that the president and his family would also die at war's end? No one has the right to send anyone to die. No one.

10. Sing Your Songs

Every 50 to 100 years, change the national anthem. It is your country only as long as you live, so why not sing an anthem that represents recent feelings, instead of what was accepted by your predecessors—and accepted only because no one else had offered a different tune?

11. The Famous Are Rich Only Because You Made Them So

Stop partaking of goods put out by actors, professional athletes and others who contribute little to society, yet are turned into national treasures. These are filthy-rich idiots who cannot even articulate a sentence in their native tongue. Listen to an actor, male or female, and you get new definitions of American English, such as "my personal friend" or "one of my best personal friends." Listen to sports figures, and their time in the spotlight would be cut in half if someone deleted their repetitious issuances of you know, you know, you know. If somebody is that stupid, why make him richer?

12. Everyone Has Ideas; Listen to Them

Every year, have a contest among all Americans offering ideas of how to make things better. The winner gets his or her name inscribed on the National Wall of Good Citizenship or some other memorial that shows those that follow that there were good people in the past.

13. Pay off the National Deficit with a Lottery

Establish a federal lottery to pay off the national debt. Each participant would contribute a set amount of dollars per workday. The money would be collected by the Social Security agency. Once a week, randomly pick one Social Security number. The weekly prize would be a single tax-free payment of $1 million. We would have to make sure that the government uses all of the money to pay off the debt. Supposedly, there are 150 million or so Americans paying

Social Security each week. If the ticket cost $10 per week and one hundred million tickets were sold, then every week the government could lessen the national deficit by $10 billion, or about $100 million per day.

14. Everybody Has a Life, Everybody Has a Story

Establish a civilian process by which each citizen can write his life experiences and have his writing deposited in a national library, so that future people can read what their predecessors felt, versus a biographer selecting the portions of a life that fit his claims.

15. Establish a Maximum Pay

Stop buying goods made by companies whose CEOs make disproportionate salaries that are thirty-forty times those of the poor slobs who work in their factories. Do this until a maximum wage is determined for the fat cats. Didn't these fat cat CEOs move the production of goods to poor countries, kept their salaries the same and give us less product for the same price? Do you really need to contribute to their wellbeing by continuing to buy their products?

16. Equal Rights for Women

Stop patronizing places or using products made by enterprises where women and men are not treated equally in pay or promotions.

17. You Cheat Me, I Don't Buy It

Again, pay attention on the contents of what you buy, and when the fat cats decrease it, but keep the price the same, stop buying it. Think about the fat cats with shelves full of unwanted products.

18. Do You Really Want to Eat Mexican Chocolate?

Stop buying products from companies that do not show the place of manufacture. One famous American chocolate company is having its chocolate made in Mexico, but on the package it just says that the well-known American company is distributing it. What next? Pork chops from Chinese pigs?

19. Stop Preening Your Lawns

Stop growing perfect lawns. Put stones in the garden, plant flowers and let the bees and the birds dine from flowers that have not been sprayed with insecticides. Get those greedy botanists and geneticists to develop ecological gardens instead of sucking up to industry to hybridize another vegetable or fruit into a tasteless mass. Stop mowing, edging and pruning your lawn with tools that are electric or driven by combustion engines. Do it by hand with human-powered tools. This would save you the gas for driving to the gym to shed your fat, you would see the results of your labor and your mind would be happier. Imagine having a maintenance-free lawn with birds nesting, bees sucking nectar and insects being eaten by birds.

20. Plant Trees in Cities

Set aside plots of land in cities and the countryside where you can buy the right to plant a tree for every child you have, with the full participation of the child. Make these plots of land immune to progress in perpetuity. Make a big deal out of it, so that as child and tree grow, there is connection to nature. Plant only trees native to the locale.

21. Identify All Sources of Pollution

Do a better job of identifying the ways we pollute, and try to decrease your contribution.

22. Legalize Prostitution

It is legal to train young people to go kill for America, and that is called patriotic. Yet sexual intercourse, the act that gave you life, is treated as profane. Can people be so dumb as not to understand that? Paying outright for intercourse, legally, is not a moral crime when contrasted with the hundreds of ways we manage to morally kill each other.

23. Make the Skies Friendly Again

Get the government to support the airlines, as it was done in the beginning. There is an old adage that I heard along the way that went like this: No one has ever made money hauling warm assholes. Now busses, subways, ferries and trains are all subsidized by local and federal governments, but commercial flying is not. This is illogical, and causes problems for those who fly as part of their employment.

24. It Is Time for Only One Child per Couple

Advocate population control, and get the population to change its attitude toward making babies. One very easy way to get the world population to less than two billion is to have only one child for each two people in their child-bearing years. Do this for three generations, and watch the number of useless abusers of nature decrease. Have the people who have made only one child or no child at all wear a special emblem to make it obvious that they care about all others. Give them support by helping them with financial problems or giving them gift certificates. The individuals who have no children should receive even more benefits.

24. Guarantee that the One Child Will Survive to Adulthood

For poor people in America and elsewhere, establish a policy that if a poor couple has only one child, and then both biological parents agree to the permanent alteration of their reproductive organs, that child will receive medical help until it reaches 18 years of age.

25. Stop Children from Having Children

Another option is to temporarily sterilize all children upon puberty, and then undo the sterilization once they have satisfied the socially established requirements to have a child. Establish child bearing rules, such as parents being at least 18 years old and having one year's salary deposited with an organization that would take over the upbringing of the child if the parents failed to do so. Parents would agree to stay together for at least 18 years to raise the child, and thereafter, disbanding the union would involve only a notarized application.

26. Sex Is Good; Let's Do It

Become more open and less puritanical about sexual matters. Allow teenagers to experiment with full warnings about diseases but none of the horrible warnings so popular when I was young. To this day, I still do not understand how an adult who has made children could have told his children that sex was dirty. Ignorance affects the lives of those who follow, so be smart, and tell it like it is.

27. Masturbation Is Good

Advocate masturbation by accepting the fact that masturbation is perhaps the easiest and most reliable sexual control tool. Of course, spread the word about all other forms of birth control, including abortion.

28. Venerate the Simple

Reject the idea that heroes are mostly people who kill other people. Venerate scientists, life-saving individuals, social scientists, writers, inventors, philosophers and people who make the world better for all. Establish a veneration of the simple people who live in poverty yet manage to live without help from others.

29. A Better Way for Reporting News

Establish a nongovernmental, popularly supported website for reporting news. Hire the top and bottom graduates from journalism schools for a two-year period. Support them with English-language editors, not subject editors, and post the stories they write on the website. You will get news coverage that is not tainted by the established news media, which are businesses with a financial, political and social agenda, and the schools get instant feedback on their students.

30. Let's See the Paper Trail

Have the government put all public records on the web. Think about this. One of your relatives died in a war. Somewhere, there is a record of the day, the battle, the place and sometimes the manner of his or her death. Would you not want to know about the last second of life of someone dear to you? I picked war because, in the end, if you see many of these horrific facts, maybe it will sway you to force your government to talk to your soon-to-be-named enemies instead of sending your child to die there.

31. Let's See the Movie

Have the government make all movies taken by any government agency made available to the public. Imagine viewing unedited movies about astronauts in space in times of pleasure and fear. Or imagine seeing your granddaddy die in battle. How will it affect those who are next in line to go die in some war dreamed up by the military industrial complex?

32. Let's Do Drugs, Legally

Legalize all drugs. Take a good portion of the taxes raised on the sale of these drugs and spend it on prevention. We haven't destroyed ourselves with alcohol or nicotine or sex; we will not destroy ourselves with drugs. Even if we did, what is the big deal? If people have so little respect for their bodies, why should society help them survive their abuses longer than they would survive unassisted? After all, if you don't have the right to commit suicide in a supposedly free American society, when will you have it?

33. Let's See the Video

Provide students with video devices instead of the notebooks and books that are presently used; it will decrease our pollution and hopefully help the students.

34. Everybody Pays the Same

Change the government taxation system to a value-added tax system in which the moment goods change hands, the government gets its share. No exceptions. Presently, the exclusion of churches from having to pay taxes shifts that burden to others, which means that all taxpayers are made to support religion. Thus, the government is saying that agnostics must support religious organizations. Where is the separation of church and state?

35. Let's Go Manual

Do you really need an electric toothbrush? Use your hand; it even helps grow better muscles in the arm. Get rid of all other electrical gadgets that you really do not need. This will lessen your burden on the environment.

36. Make All Batteries Recyclable

Batteries, when put in landfills, do not convert to chemicals that are useful to the soil. Recycle them.

37. Women—Be Real instead of Beauty Contestants

Do women really need all the chemicals that are found in their makeup and body creams? For what purpose do women put on makeup other than that everyone else is doing it? What if women were educated on the waste of time, energy and pollution created by such selfish acts as having too much clothing and makeup?

38. The Gun Issue Is Solved; Next

Assume that reason prevails and gun regulations are changed so that the hunters and sport shooters keep their guns. What do you think would be the next problem? The possibilities include drugs, alcohol, drivers, pollution, population and poverty. No matter what the next problem is after resolving the gun dilemma, there will always be problems. If Americans can resolve the gun problem, then the new issues may be easier to solve since most of them do not have constitutional rooting.

39. Think about the Energy

Men should stop shaving and getting labor-intensive haircuts. Just get a trim with scissors each month. Take the time, the chemicals and the energy involved in the making of the tools with which you shave and cut your hair and ask yourself why.

40. Respect Brown People

If the well-being of humanity had been a universal human goal during the last century, *aka the century of wars*, these people would have done more toward that end than anyone else: Gandhi, Martin Luther King Jr., Mandela, Mother Theresa. Three of these were brown skinned. Isn't it sad that whereas whites have produced Einstein, Fermi, Bohr, Newton and hundreds of others who performed miracles in science, the brown-skinned people did more for humanity than the scientists? If going to sleep at night without fear is important, then the brown-skinned people outdid the whites.

41. Are You Really an Individual?

Most of the things you do were done by the majority and are thoughtless habits passed down to your replacements. For example, we wear neckties because everyone else wears ties. This supposedly started when a group of Croatian soldiers working for Napoleon marched down a Parisian street wearing some type of scarf. The ladies started dressing their men in these scarves and began to call them cravats, which was derived from the word Croat. Today, we choke during the working hours in that stupid portable noose because that is the style. That is conformity for you. If you stopped wearing a tie, are your body and mind still useful to someone who needs your services? Get rid of them. And for the sake of humanity, don't start exposing your chest hair as a balancing act to the present way women expose their breasts at work.

42. Let's Praise the Ones Who Help Us All

Establish a week-long celebration of the deeds of great humans. Select them on the basis of what they did for humanity versus how they destroyed humanity or nature. Set up a system similar to the Nobel Prize, except that people throughout the world would select those to be honored each year. It would not allow deeds involving politicians or military, but all other aspects of humanity and nature would be considered. Erect a statue to each individual selected each year. Imagine seeing or learning about Isaac Newton's contributions instead of hearing "Jailhouse Rock" or the present music heard from the dens of the young?

43. Lower Your Pollution Factor

Establish a scale to measure the pollution-generating factor for humans, animals and man-made processes. Call it whatever is acceptable to the masses, but for this purpose, I will call it the Human

Ecological Scale, with units of HES. It is a measure of how much energy you use to live and how much pollution is caused by the conversion of that energy.

a. The person who lives on the street would have an abnormally low HES number, while the leader of a country, a CEO, or a rich person would achieve the highest HES ratings. A basketball player would have a lower HES number than a football player. Just look at the bodies and equipment involved.

b. I am 230 lbs. of walking matter that is kept at 98.6°F. Since I am 70.0 lbs. overweight, I am likely using enough extra energy to keep a pre-teen alive. But that is not all. I like to cook and even cook on the grill. How much extra energy do I use in doing that versus eating a room-temperature can of pork and beans? I also need TVs, music, a truck that gets 22 miles to the gallon at best, my beer and wine, my lawn and gardening equipment and my fishing gear. My medicine and medical care not only drain money from the others on my insurance plan, but the making of these drugs uses energy and causes pollution. I also need bigger clothes than I would need if I were normal weight. Each of these factors would have an HES rating.

c. People would know their HES rankings based on some logical summation of these individual factors. Don't despair. Bookkeepers have changed accounting so that an employer can even estimate how much toilet paper to buy for the crew. Computing human energy consumption should not break new ground in accounting.

d. On a scale of 0–100 HES, I would probably rate in the 90 HES range. A dead person in an unmarked and untended grave would probably rate 0 HES. Of course, this would lead people to think that heating a mansion is against nature. Perhaps a young woman would not learn to put makeup on her body because she would conform to the new fad. Think of the possible ramifications and the ways people could be charmed into following it, so that they would become more environmentally compatible.

44. We, the Old, Should Die at the First Chance We Get

The concept that we, the old, must live until some vital organ fails, even after years of helping it along with medicine, is an artificial concept. When not tended by humans, all other things in nature live and die according to natural events. If we, the lingering-on and old farts, truly wanted to help with the well-being of all, we would never accept an option to live a few more years while our minds and bodies rot.

Here is what we can do. This concept should be used only for people who have reasonable minds and have lived a long time. It must never be made into a law, but it should never be impeded by laws.

  a. Presently, the only options available to humans who acknowledge that their bodies are slowly breaking down are to take better care of their bodies and ingest medicines to delay the inevitable death. Though you may want to die, everything is aimed at keeping you alive. The hypocrisy of waiting for death to come on a deathbed is best exemplified by the same human minds who put their pet to sleep. Out of good will a sick dog is killed on the vets' table, a decision made by humans. Yet a human being must be allowed to suffer till the organs just give up. But process of keeping a human alive is illogical when looked at it from a religious aspect. If no medicine had been used, that human would be dead, as some believe to be the will of God. But man interfered and put medicine into the moribund body, and then man reaches a quandary where he feels it a sin to stop giving the medicine to the dying person. By your beliefs you interfered in a process initiated by your God, and now that you messed it up, you give the problem back to God?

b.   Here is a nice and thoughtful way out. When a human reaches a point in life—let's do the numbers and say between 35 and 55 years—there is usually enough wisdom accumulated for the person to finally understand that he or she has begun the descent toward death. There is also a logical acceptance of the fact that your body is dying. This should be the time to draw up a legal document that states at what point on your moribund trip you want to die. The reason for this age bracket is to prevent you from entering the rationalization stage where you accept corporal failures because you can easily compare yourself to contemporaries and make stupid rationalizations, such as, "Yeah, I wear diapers, but at least I can still walk; Marylou uses a wheelchair, and she is two years younger than I am."

c.   Each human who is so willing would fill out a quality of life document. The individual has sole responsibility for the items to be included and the value to allocate to each item. After the document is complete, the human could have up to five years to change it or cancel it totally. Before the document could become effective, the person would be required to discuss it with five trusted people who are not necessarily friends or family but who are people who could execute the document.

d.   As an example, here is what a malfunction table would be like:

MY QUALITY OF LIFE TABLE

MALFUNCTION	ASSIGNED VALUE (%)
Loss of mental functions	100
Loss of body functions, incontinence, and so on.	60
Loss of ambulatory functions	20
Unable to see	10
Loss of sex drive	50
Heart problems	50
Inability to feed oneself	40
Desire to die	100

I have picked for myself a cumulative failure value of 60 percent. When the total of each assigned malfunction reaches 60 percent, the show is over for me.

As an adult, you could prevent becoming an unwanted child to your children. You have seen what it is like to deal with old parents and grandparents before they are brought to the dying houses. Why not prevent that shameful phase of your life? I do not believe any government has the right to make you live as some older folks are made to live. Rather, I should have the right to get one last sexual fantasy, a good bottle of red wine and a naked vixen reading me passages out of *Fanny Hill* while I swallow the eternal sleeping pill.

Before you start pontificating the crap out of this, please visit old people in the dying houses that pass as retirement homes, or wipe your mom's ass or give her a bath, or go to a death house, so nicely called hospices, and imagine yourself there. Why not allow those of us who want to die with some shreds of remaining self-respect to have our way? You can die with pride instead of shame, and if you currently respect yourself, you will understand the importance of that. If not, no one will try to convince you otherwise.

This process cannot be used by people who are mentally challenged. They must be kept alive by whatever means society has developed, since it would be murder otherwise. Yes, this means that the prince with no brains could not opt for this option.

45. Bury the Cemeteries

Another element of death that we can change to ease the burden of our presence on the environment involves altering the environmentally abusive process of using cemeteries. Is there really a reason to cut the grass that grows on graves for a century or two before the money runs out for this upkeep, or someone steals the headstones, or the trees take over the land again? Do you really see any benefits in national military cemeteries other than continuing the crap about the nobility of young men dying for their country, while we, the elders, live on? Think of it this way; where are the cemeteries of the Crusaders? Or the cemeteries of the French Legionnaires who died in Indochina?

To curb the environmental damage caused by preserving the memories of ourselves, we, those who are about to die, should be given another option of a more ecological burial. This burial will consist of your naked remains being picked up and wrapped in a biodegradable cloth and then buried in an unmarked grave with six to twelve other corpses. The burial site would be unmarked and no efforts made to keep the local flora from turning the gravesites into wilderness. Then, while the burial is taking place, your relatives can go have one great party on whatever credit cards you left behind. Of course, this has to be done before the credit card people are notified about your death.

Imagine doing good for society even after you are dead by opting for a burial spot that has trees providing oxygen, shelter for fauna, and greenery for those who follow. Your deeds during life may be forgotten, but you will be remembered in death by your last ecological effort.

46. Stick with Ecology; It Will Help All

Here are some other ecological steps that you can take:

a. Start walking instead of using a vehicle, and if you need to drive, share trips with neighbors. Walking will also provide you with exercise.

b. Flying uses more energy than any other form of transportation, which causes more pollution. Ask yourself whether your trip is really worth the pollution it generates.

c. Coincidentally, this will also show the US government that you were not the one who caused 9/11 or will cause another such event. In your refusal to use planes, you will also shun the machines that outline your naked body to the minimum wage morons who pat you down.

d. Do we really need the hundreds of magazines that we leaf through in the waiting rooms of so many facilities? Instead, we should equip waiting rooms with video screens void of any advertisements.

e. Sending unsolicited paper catalogs means that trees are cut down and the chemicals that are used to make the paper are emptied into rivers, just so someone can make a buck. Instead, provide catalogs online and e-mails alerts to potential customers.

f. Food packaging and display on store shelves has gotten out of hand. This should be decreased and companies should standardize packages. One way to achieve this is to stamp numbers on plain boxes. Each container would be made of materials that rot in less than six months when disposed of, and have the name of the manufacturer, a number, a name in multiple languages, and the contents. The shopping carts could have scanners and screens where the contents and all other pertinent data about the product can be displayed. Imagine how much less pollution there would be without so much colored paint and fancy plastic boxes that don't rot?

g. Imagine having a display on your shopping cart that will tell you how much it is going to cost and how many fats, calories, carbs, fiber, and unnecessary chemicals you have in the cart as you go down the aisles.

h. Install solar-powered video cameras with audio in national parks and have them online all the time. Do this for waterfalls, in nesting areas for birds, scenic sections of rivers, and, of course, underwater, so that many can see those fish that may soon disappear. People can watch them live on the video screens in their homes, thus saving the energy involved in getting to the parks, and not physically interfering with the so-called wild side of nature. Imagine how nature would appreciate your staying out of her way?

i. Establish different working shifts so traffic and total electrical energy usage can be kept at lower levels. Humans could survive with fewer highway lanes and less power generation. If you moved a good percentage of the workers to the night shift, you would need fewer electric plants, less roads and employ more people.

j. It is time to move on to bidets or some other water-based way of cleaning yourself after using the commode. The idea of using soft paper is a very big burden on nature.

Cull the energy saving ideas that live in the minds of the millions of people that make up this earth, and you will have less pollution.

47. Stop Celebrating Failure

Again, I detest the recent establishment of celebratory periods in recognition of past misdeeds. The month of February, to mention one, is dedicated to recognizing the various contributions of different races. You can't undo the damage that was created by three to four centuries of slavery by celebrating the coexistence of races during February. You can, however, publicly display admission of the wrongs, and then establish programs that train, mentor, guide, assist with employment, provide mental help and give pride to the children of minorities.

In America and worldwide, the attitude toward the poor is the most shameful trait of humankind. Even more diabolic is the way the rich think of the poor. Once in a while, a poor person breaks the barriers and achieves, and the rich people say, "See, you can achieve if you try." This is the most self-serving crap ever dished out by society. In other countries, they still have caste systems and people are suppressed. In a way, that hopeless state may be less disturbing than giving people false hope.

48. Celebrations for the Peaceful Ones

There is a great need to give people common goals, and thus make all realize that we, the self-proclaimed best thing that happened in the realm of the animal world, can live in a better environment. Every year, we should have an international peace week. We would stop normal life and have festive events for one week, but only in countries that did not participate in any war during the previous year. Switzerland would run this operation since there is no other developed country, I think, with a longer peaceful existence. We would only do this in countries that do not have the death penalty or where the citizenry is not violent, as is the case in America.

49. Take the prayer out of Tax-Sponsored Places

Take away all signs of religion from the government functions and premises, coins and paper money, and from the public schools.

50. Do Some Foreign Policy of Your Own

Do not sell or buy any products to/from countries that are occupying other countries or lands that belonged to others. If you did this, it would mean that China would stop exporting its products to all until it pulled out of Tibet, or Israel would pull out of the lands that it is trying to populate. Think about it.

51. Make English a Logical Lingo

Establish, if possible, a logical language, a language that is immune to multiple interpretations and that cannot be questioned by any lawyer. People would be allowed to use any language they wish, but if one person were to specify that the answers to his or her questions must be in the logical language, it would decrease ambiguity and lying. This could lead to fewer arguments, shootings and lawyers.

52. AMA + Americans = Pill Poppers

Help the American Medical Association grow up and start training its doctors in simple things like:

    a. A headache is a big deal. It is a better body status indicator than body temperature, so stop minimizing it. If the brain makes its container manifest pain, it is serious. It is something like a firehouse being on fire and the firefighters being told that it is a minor issue.

b. Get rid of outdated words like malaria and flu. These are a continuation of the lore and witchcraft of centuries ago. Use their medical definitions.

c. When the doctor enters the examination room, he or she should be prohibited from asking, "How are you?" If the patient is not sick, why is he there? Instead, ask, "And what is ailing you today?"

d. The drug makers and the AMA have entered an illicit affair, and this has made doctors overmedicate every patient. We have pharmacies at every corner and more going up. If this is good, I will go along with it, but in the end, what good is it to society to keep people like me alive?

53. Practice Civil Obedience

In the first 12 to 14 years of schooling, teach civil obedience to all students. As students progress, ensure that they have an unmistakable understanding of legal and illegal behavior. Point out that movies that show killing and the abuse of others are showing what *not* to do in real life. For the class trip, put them in a prison, and let them savor the life that could be theirs. Once students graduate, they would be tested and receive citizenship and enjoy all of the benefits of the laws of the land, including drinking, smoking, whoring, and whatever else is required by youths.

By formally teaching the young their responsibilities within a society, you would be give the power of knowledge, knowledge that has never been taught in the family environment. If it had, why is there crime and corruption throughout the world, as there has always been? How else can you explain the continuation of war, hate, prejudice, killing and starvation without understanding that we fail to arm our replacements with codes of behavior? If a citizen graduates and then breaks the law, the punishment should be, for a first offense, six to 12 months of concentrated mental, physical and legal retraining. Castration, tubal ligation and lobotomy should be considered for the incorrigibles. The lobotomy and castration must leave the individual able to hold menial jobs but unable to contrive criminal schemes or bring offspring into society.

54. One More Time

Again, legalize all drugs used for pleasure and entertainment. Use the tax revenues from this act to establish schools and agencies similar to Alcoholics Anonymous to teach the detriments of doing drugs. There are two reasons that would convince even the dullest American to go this route. The first is that people will do what they want to do; Prohibition proved that. The second is that if you want to help decrease the crime rates of Central-American countries and in American streets, the best way to do it is to remove the present illegal supply and furnish drugs to those who want them.

55. Work from Home

If you don't need to be physically present at your designated workplace, convince your leaders that you can work from home. You save time, you save money, and you help save the earth.

56. Railroads are Cheaper than Airlines

Get local governments to invest in better rail transportation. It is the least-polluting form of mass transportation other than walking.

57. Our History Has Legends and Skips the Bad We Did

Have the history books of each country written by other countries. This should be done on a randomly selected basis. This is the only way that the nationalistic crap will stop and a more truthful history emerges about each country. Every nation has periods of misbehavior.

Europe had its inquisition; then, they came to the Americas and killed. America had its slaves, its witches, the slaughter of the Native Americans, the mistreatment of Jews, Irish, Italians, Asian Americans, and today, the Latinos. Basically, we are all evil, some or most of the time, so just make sure this trait of ours is told to all who come after us and is told as accurately and nakedly as it can be told.

58. All Should Speak, Fluently, another Language

Have all children learn a foreign language in school, and toward the end of mandatory schooling, have the youngster live in the country that uses that language for an entire school year. The youngster should live with poor people so that he or she understands how these people live. We should also establish a pen pal system, so that the youngster must use the language to communicate with another youngster. For example, an Arabic-speaking child would write in English to an American child who is learning Arabic. The American child would answer in Arabic. Each child would correct the other's writings. Mandate at least one letter per week for each child.

59. Make Pen Pal Friends with the World

As adults, have citizens of one nation communicate with citizens of others, so that if there is communication between the common people, perhaps they will be brave enough to refuse to go kill their overseas friends.

60. Make another Race

In America, the WASP immigrants that arrived one hundred or two hundred or even four hundred years ago seem to have adopted the attitude that they are better than those who arrived later. There is a way to stop the inherent discrimination that has been a way of life with the established WASPs. The best and easiest way to do it is to intermarry. Just advocate intermarriage until America becomes brown or gold instead of black or white. Once that is accomplished in about two to three generations, the ones who decided to remain pure WASPs will be a minority, and we can let the chips fall where they may.

61. End Race Selection

When President Obama calls himself black, I believe he is wrong. He is multiracial. Why, then, is he calling himself black? But think about this; what if all black Americans did away with the idea that they were black? Biologically, we are the same, and after a person admits to being black, it is, in a sense, the beginning of bad things to come. Assume that black Americans, like black people the world over, instead just went about their business and never claimed to be black? If asked for their race, they would answer, "human." If we take away artificial designations of color, then perhaps we can start to treat each as equals, just as we are biologically. Try it.

62. Let's All Do It the Same Way

Make the following changes apply to all nations:

a. Standardize the designation of dates. It should be: hour, day, month, year.

b. Change the designation of time from the present a.m./p.m. system to the twenty-four-hour clock.

c. Change the decimal referencing system. The Europeans use the comma, while the Americans use the period to denote the same thing. Use one or the other.

63. Mothers of Dead Soldiers Talk to Each Other

Convince the mothers of dead soldiers, including the mothers of dead terrorists and dead guerilla fighters, and, of course, the mothers whose children were killed as a function of collateral damage, to start an organization to share their grief and create a more peaceful world. These women would have the deepest desire to prevent other mothers from suffering as they are suffering, which could make us stop going to war so often.

64. End Collateral Damage

American wars destroy everything in the path of American forces to minimize casualties and stimulate our economic production of war goods. This razing of the battlefield just happens to kill civilians. With our typical unemotional buzzwords, we call civilians killed collateral damage. To the sufferers of this collateral damage, the term has a different meaning. It means total disrespect for humanity and the production of more hate and revenge to come. Let's hope that you, the replacements, can approach all humanity with un-bloodied hands and true hearts instead of our American way of killing them all to establish democracy. If you cannot do that, then don't try to act civilized when your ways are so shallow that you address the killing of unarmed civilians as collateral damage. I am ashamed that I chose to be an American when those words are spoken.

65. Free the Women

In most civilizations, women have accepted subhuman roles that range from slavery in some sects of the Muslim religion to child-breeding machines in polygamous religious sects in America. Those who think this subservient status of women is deserved because women should have rebelled against it suffer from superficial views and poorly reasoned conclusions. Under abusive government, women, like men, will make do with many intolerable conditions solely for fear of death. Humans are, after all, content to have food and a warm place to eat and shit it, and then sleep. How else do you explain the Cubans that remained home under the Castro regime? Awaken all to the simple fact that humans are not to be imprisoned by anyone or any ideology.

Servitude is servitude, no matter what religious or ethnic blanket it is wrapped in.

66. We Killed, We Failed, Now Please Stop

Americans need to stop the democratization of the world. Here are some results of our spreading of democracy, which only kills people and leaves behind more hatred for Americans:

a. After decades of Americanization in the Philippines, we left behind a corrupt country where young Catholic girls leave their native land to become whores the world over. Oh, let me tell you about the first redneck professor that I ever met. During a history lecture, this professor said that during the independence ceremony of the Philippines, one of their officials supposedly said, "If you are to be colonized, it is best to be colonized by the Americans." Of course, the fellow did not really have the freedom to say what he felt, so it was not his fault. But this professor's point was that America was a good colonizer. As I began to understand the world for what it was, I finally figured out that the professor was wrong. In reality, the Filipino official said nothing more than that if you are going to get raped, it is best if you get raped by a fellow with a small dick. Colonizing a country, whether it is done by America, Iraq or Israel is simple subjugation of the natives. That is as wrong today as it was one thousand years ago.

b. Central America, Cuba, Panama, Bolivia and other countries that we either occupied or sent Marines in to get our way are not democracies.

c. Japan, Korea, Vietnam, Iraq, Afghanistan and Iran are by no means democracies. Then again, is America really a democracy or a mostly pacified nation of citizens who are obese, uneducated, xenophobic and less interested in where we send our young to die than in what is happening on TV?

67. Once Again, Elect Women

I am still trying to convince you to elect women, ASAP. Female servitude is not just the overt abuse of women dictated by various religions. It lives in many other forms. Here is what happened to women in America, which is supposedly the best democracy created by men. During the first two centuries of America's existence, its politicians sent one to two million citizens to die in declared and undeclared wars. Women made these young men who died, but the mothers never participated in making those decisions. During the existence of America, there have been roughly fifteen thousand congressmen and maybe three hundred congresswomen. What if we switch from the present composition of male-dominated leadership to a per capita basis? Think about females making decisions about whether their sons and daughters should go die for a plot of sand, or some oil or for people that would not know democracy if you gave it to them on a silver platter.

68. No Discounts for Anyone

Make all discounts based on age or employment status illegal. If our wage system is fair, then everybody can use the money as they wish, but no one should have privileges.

69. Honor Children

Establish a week-long period for honoring children. In the end, you will need the children more than they will need you. You remember that some of them, the ones you called useless, will be the ones who will wipe your ass when you are older. The brighter ones will make your life easier. And when you are old, like those morons who went before, you will also use the cliché that the kids of today suck. So, honor them while they are carefree youths because once they grow up, they can be like you, or perhaps, with a bit of love and mentoring, they will be better than you.

70. Keep Your Finger to Yourself

Change the licensing of drivers to include more schooling and better driving practices, and make the cost of licenses much higher. Use the extra money to repair and build roads. If properly done, this will decrease our accident rates and will also make the drivers less spontaneous with their opinions when someone else makes a mistake. If a license is suspended, drivers would repeat the licensing process, thus making all drivers think twice about pulling stunts on the road and showing their IQ with their extended digit.

71. Jury Trials Should Not Be Amateur Thespians at Work

Give people who are to be tried in courts the option of being tried by three judges instead of undergoing what is nothing more than showmanship in the present jury selection and theatrical trial system. The saying is true that if you are tried by a jury, you are being judged by a group of people who were not even smart enough to get out of jury duty. Choose the three judges; it will take less time, less acting, less crap and you will have the best chance of going free if you really did not do it.

72. How Much Less Can I Eat?

Have the government develop a simpler and more realistic set of dietary recommendations, including a critical scientific assessment of pills and cures sold by the billions by pill mongers. In America, the greed for money causes millions of people with marginal thinking abilities to waste millions on pills, diets and other cures for everything from limp dicks to fat asses to looking older than you think you should. These poor people who grab at any straw to look like the superhumans depicted in the ads should be protected. In case a redneck is reading this, think of it this way; if you educate Elvira about nutrition and diets that work, she will not need that electric stroller at Walmart. This means that you will not have to bitch under your breath about her blocking the aisles, taking wide turns, or even worse, backing up. You will also pay a bit less at checkout and in insurance fees and taxation if she is educated to actually maintain her weight. Of course, you know she is on welfare, but then again, she is white, so how can that be? Right?

73. Show us the Three out of Four Doctors

When research facilities report findings, they should also have to report the names and amounts of money given by all contributors.

74. Stop Paying to Watch Commercials

You are watching TV, and though you are paying for the cable that brings the program, the vendor feels it is fair to bombard you with commercials. This is wrong. The TV is yours, the house is yours, and you are paying the sons of bitches for bringing the program into your house. Here is one possible way to stop this. Have the government order broadcasters to codify the stuff coming into your cable or satellite dish. Then make program to blank out commercials, infomercials and so on. This would leave the door open to those sneaky bastards who invite an author to promote his or her book under the guise of an interview. But you will at least have the a worthwhile freedom, unless you are the fellow who keeps those snake oil vendors in business. Another possibility is to have a rating system of each channel that shows how many hours of commercials/religion are broadcast per day.

75. Help Me Open the Thick, Plastic Package

Force all product packaging to be made in such a way that an arthritic granny can open it. The heavy, clear, plastic packaging that supposedly keeps the thieves away also seems to cut your hands when you try to open the darn thing at home. You should not need box cutters or scissors to open a plastic container. If you want to convince everyone that they should stop doing this to you, then have the store open it. Few days later, return it. Duplicate this a few thousand times, and the store people will do the required bitching to the suppliers, and the packaging will be changed. This, like speed bumps on public roads and searching at airports, is an illegal abuse. If you are paying for something, why should you be made to suffer while opening it? The simple answer is that no one gives a damn about you, including you.

76. Get a Job with the Federal Government

In America, some people are better than others. Here is an example of this, and you pay for it without ever being aware of it. Assume that you work for the US government as a civilian employee with 15 years of seniority. Here is what your employment benefits would be. The US government says that a work year is 2,087 hours long. If you were paid every two weeks, you would work ten days for every paycheck, or a total of 260 days per year. An employee who has worked fifteen or more years with the government gets 26 days of vacation, or one day for every two weeks; 13 days of sick leave, or four hours every two weeks; and 13 holidays. This means 52 paid days off each year. Since your work year is 260 days, you would only have to work 208 days, or 1,664 hours, to get the pay for 260 days, or 2,087 hours.

In other words, you get 5.2 paychecks without showing up at work. You work 80 percent of the time and you get 100 percent of the pay. If it snows, civil servants get a partial or full day off. They are too delicate to go to work on dangerous roads.

All of this is paid by you, the nongovernment type taxpayers. How much vacation do you get? Two weeks per year to be used for sick leave or vacation? If you stay home because of the weather, do you get paid? Now how is it that a civil servant is treated better than you, and you are paying for it? Your servants are getting a better deal than you. What a wonderful reversal of roles. By the way, you will probably find a virgin in a whorehouse before you find a federal worker telling you that he is overpaid and has too many benefits. Don't you think it is time to rebel against this crap?

In my opinion, the majority of white civil servant camp followers that I have encountered were rednecks. They spend at least couple hours per day chatting, searching the web, enjoying long lunches, and so on. In rare sober conversations some of them admit that they would never pay a worker for the work they are being paid to do. Yet these same people, who usually think of themselves as the truest Americans, will let you know in disguised ways that America is going to hell because of minorities sucking on the drying tit of America.

77. Don't Let Your Government Treat You Like a Dummy

Politicians are more apt to create a catchy phrase than to use simple English to tell us that they are confused and hope their new solution works. Through the years, here are some of the rallying cries that our juvenile leaders left for us:

Whip inflation now: You've got to be old to know that one

Trickle-down economics: That was based on the theory of the dog begging for food under the table. Whatever trickled down was yours.

No child left behind: This one was sound, except that they left the counting to other politicians.

We're as mad as hell and we're not going to take it anymore! This actually came from a movie, but was co-opted by the politicians.

These clichés of the simple legislative and executive branch minds should be forever inscribed on a monument of stupidity located next to their workplaces. It certainly would help all Americans to understand when they have been deceived by buffoons and their cheerleaders.

78. Johnny, You Cannot Have a Pet Until...

No child under a certain age should be allowed to have a dog, cat, bird, or whatever else unless he or she is deemed qualified. In order to be qualified to have a pet, the youngster should put in a minimal amount of time working at an animal shelter to determine their true understanding of the commitments involved.

79. One Senator for Thirteen Million?

There are seven states in America that each have over ten million residents. There are 26 states that each have fewer than five million residents. I understand fully the roles of representatives and senators, and there is an assumed difference between what a representative can do for you and what a senator can do for you. But the state populations of 1776 aren't comparable to those of today. They have changed logarithmically. It is still disproportionate, however. In the state of California, two senators represent roughly 38 million residents, or 24 million each. In Delaware, South Dakota, Alaska, North Dakota, Vermont and Wyoming, the two senators in each state have fewer than 1million residents to attend to. Is it really as simple as this? Assume that any restaurant in America was forced to have only two cooks but could have a standardized ratio of servers to tables. Where would you get better service, in a small town or big city restaurant?

80. Getting Your Goat

We should do a study to see which type of animal creates the least pollution during the process of sending a pound of cooked meat to a table. If getting an eight-ounce beef steak to your table causes twice as much pollution as the same amount of lamb, pork, goat, chicken or rabbit, you could still have your steak, but you would have to pay an ecological damage fee.

81. What is an Alien?

Redefine the rights of alien residents in America and enforce them. For example, is it really OK to insinuate that Omar was born in America but is not as American as Clyde from West Virginia because Omar's mommy and daddy were from an Arabic country?

82. Stop Blaming the Media

There are many people, the marginals, who feel that the media in America is responsible for their problems. In reality, there are media outlets that cater to conservatives and to liberals. The marginals are deficient in their selection. When somebody sings a different tune than the one they wish to hear, they get upset. Can someone tell these idiots that if you want to learn something, you must deal with those who have different views than your own? Or they could turn to a media outlet that marches to their tune.

83. Listen to Yourself

Stop using stupid words to ease the acts they represent. Saying that Betty Lou passed away is stupid. She died, and there was no passing involved. You don't put down a dog or a horse, you kill it. Southern belles perspire, while southern men sweat. How cute, and how silly. The people at the scene of a natural disaster are not observing decimation. Decimation is only a 10 percent loss. When the tornado came through the town and destroyed it, it did not decimate it; it *centinnated* it. My attempt at getting Webster to add a new word to the dictionary.

84. Walk it Off

Every evening or whenever your end of the day is, go for a half-hour walk, rain or shine, and clear your mind of the deeds of the day. Do not watch TV, and by so doing, you will mess up their demographics.

85. Prison or Rehabilitation, Make a Decision

To fill our prison with so many people and pay for their upkeep is pure stupidity. Either make prisons places of rehabilitation, in which case the ex-con should be given a new name and clean record when he or she is released, or put a new amendment in the Constitution stating that people sentenced to a term of life without parole lose all constitutionally guaranteed rights and must be fed and clothed by their families. We are driven to rehabilitate and preserve the constitutional rights of people who will never see freedom again. You just can't have it both ways. This is not a novel approach. We already kill murderers, and if that is not taking away someone's constitutional rights, I don't know what would be.

86. Keep the TSA Out of My Pants

Admit that airport searches are an invasion of privacy and stop them. Change the laws so that all relatives of the perpetrators of air piracy will be killed, including their children and spouses. The deed should be advertised. Kill as many relatives as were killed in the crime the fellow committed. Try this for a test period and see what happens to terrorism. Of course, this would also have to be applied to our leaders when they decide to go on their own and invade countries or kill people in undeclared wars.

87. Give up on the Heavenly Virgins

The horrible people that recruit marginal humans to do their bidding in war must allow this new recruit to receive sexual favors from family members of the recruiter. This will achieve four things:

a. The soon-to-be suicide bomber gets laid by a relative of the recruiter, on earth, just in case the 22 virgins or whatever do not materialize after his death. Remember—religions only promise you things after you are dead, so why take a chance on sex?

b. The recruiter learns that he does have a personal involvement in the deed.

c. The soon-to-be suicide bomber may not like sex and decide to continue living.

d. After trying sex with opposites, it may be that the suicide bomber-to-be does not like females; he will need a guarantee that he will find 22 male virgins up there.

Also, a suicide bomber would think twice if he knew that upon completion of the act, their entire family would be exterminated. Go for what is dear to the killers. Parents and relatives would pay attention to what their children are thinking and doing, if only to save their own lives.

88. Stop Allowing them to Treat America as a Whore

America is nothing more than a whore in the hearts and minds of politicians. Think about the way America gets treated:

a. George Bush Sr. picked Dan Quayle as a vice-president. That was nothing more than a test. If Americans were so stupid as to pick Danny boy, the daddy would know that Americans were stupid enough to pick his son, the prince with no brains. There was no interest in giving America the best possible candidate; the ploy was simply to establish another American potentate.

b. But the whoredom did not stop there. Ross Perot emerged, and though his commercial abilities merit study, the poor political moron picked Stockdale as a vice-presidential candidate. If there was anything more insulting to the poor man and to the nation, I do not know of it. Mr. Stockdale was a very honorable man, but he let greed take over and fell from being a hero to an also-ran. Sad, ain't it? If you really respected America, would you do that to her? Would you pick an idiot like Dan Quayle to be a heartbeat away from the presidency? Worse yet, would you insult an otherwise noble American like Stockdale by putting him on your ticket because you needed a war hero?

c. And the whoredom didn't stop there either. There was once a moron from Pascagoula, MS, who came within four heartbeats of being a president. You didn't know that about Trent Lott did you? Then there was Sarah, she could have made it as a Playboy centerfold but instead was picked by dummy McCain to be one heartbeat away from the presidency. Of course, there was the Gipper and the Crook and Spiro the Greek-shamer.

If that is not pimping America, I do not know what would be. Elicit the people of this nation to respect it and develop an election process that stops the feces from rising to the top as if they were cream. America deserves better than what she has been dealt.

89. Understand, We Are Humans Who Err

Teach the young that those who went before them did make mistakes, and teach them how to analyze and learn from those mistakes. This can be easily done if the elders admit to their errant ways instead of shirking the blame. We could accomplish this easily if each country's history books were written by people from other nations. For example, Winston Churchill was deemed such a hero that he was even given an honorary American citizenship, even though he was responsible for the fiasco of Gallipoli and acted the same in Norway in World War II. He pushed for the invasion of Italy, and what a fiasco that turned out to be. It took 18 months to travel from Sicily to the Po valley. Hannibal took less time to travel the same distance using elephants. Then, of course, there was the great American field marshal, Douglas MacArthur, who wasted the lives of tens of thousands of people by invading the Philippines for no reason other than wanting to "return."

The sad thing is that the misdeeds of the higher-ups are hidden for decades and then publicized only by interested writers. History should be truthful and accurate, and crap like the 300 Greeks of Thermopylae should never have been put in history books. The number was ten times higher. How can one lie in history books? If there is anything sacred, would it not be recorded history?

90. Study Switzerland

A long time ago, in a debate aboard a Navy ship, I suggested to what turned out to be a true-blue, American redneck that Americans should study the ways of the Swiss. The Swiss have managed to stay out of wars for hundreds of years amid neighbors who could do nothing else but kill each other every 20 years or so. The dumb son of a bitch responded by saying, "Yeah, Switzerland has stayed out of wars, but what have they invented, the Swiss army knife?" I got the gist quickly and responded, "You mean to tell me that five hundred thousand dead Americans beginning with World War II was a fair price for us to get radar, jet planes and cable TVs?" The bastard looked confused.

91. I Did Not Cause the Accident, So Make Way

Traffic jams caused by accidents are inexcusable. Those hurt or killed in the incident do not automatically assume higher values than the thousands stuck in the jam created by at least one of the people involved in the accident. States should develop better means to quickly document the incident and push the disabled vehicles off the road. Put a couple traffic directors on the scene to direct the traffic onto the road shoulder if necessary. Just get the traffic moving. These are people who have no fault in the incident and are causing excess pollution because of the inabilities of others.

92. *Foison* for all

America, because of its natural wealth and consumerism, is in a never-ending *foison,* or rich harvest. Though we enjoy the bounty of the land and the creations of those ingenious minds among us, we fail terribly to understand that there is a world out there. We not only claim but actually feel that we are always the best, the first, the infallible. In reality, we are mostly strugglers on the ladder of life, but fool ourselves into believing that we are perched at the top and cannot be bumped. Here is a little reality:

a. The residents of Herculaneum had running water in their houses before 79 AD. In Italy, in 1955 we had an inside bathroom with a commode and a pail of water to flush it. In Vietnam the USAF had flushing toilets, while the US Army had shacks with cut up 55 gallon drums receiving your droppings. Fuel was poured on them and the feces were burned. In case you need to see how they did it, there is an accurate scene in the movie *Platoon.* We used to think it was done that way so that on calm days the black columns of smoke gave the VC targeting references.

b. I lived in Virginia Beach for about 20 years and had three bathrooms in my house, with running water. But when I traveled 50 to 100 miles away on Virginia State Route 58, I would see outhouses with grassless paths leading from the houses.

c. The space race between America and the Soviet Union was actually a race between two groups of German space scientists who had been caught accidentally by the two countries. The Soviet Union and America contributed the means, but the brains were German. Unknown to many, there was an American by the name of Goddard who tried to interest our military in rocketry but failed. When he talked to Hitler's' boys, they listened, or so the story goes.

d. American history, movies and books make America the sole winner of World War II. It just so happens that these countries were also involved: England, France, Russia, Australia, Belgium, Bolivia, Brazil, Canada, China, Denmark, Greece, Mexico, The Netherlands, New Zealand, Norway, Poland, South Africa and Yugoslavia.

e. We have more computers than the rest of the world put together, yet we cannot develop a tamper- and error-proof voting machine.

f. We cannot stop or decrease crime; we just respond to the killings.

g. Americans actually believe that ethnic food eaten in America is the real thing, when, in reality, it is not even a distant third cousin to the foods eaten in Mexico, China or Italy.

h. Americans overseas stand out like bulls in a china closet when it comes to being respectful of the ways of the natives.

i. In Vietnam, the Military Assistance Command, Vietnam, had combat troops count the number of dead enemies. Toward the end of the war, someone asked the simple question of whether we are killing more men than were being born in North Vietnam. The answer was no. The military stopped counting. So the story goes.

j. Our educational system is most likely the costliest in the world, yet if you watch the street interviews that Jay Leno conducts, you will conclude that your well-considered reasons for voting for a specific candidate are cancelled by morons.

The list of our ineptitudes is much longer, but because of our wealth and our isolationism, we are the best at being the bullies of the world. No one can top us when it comes to running down the halls of this earth and bombing this little guy and that little guy. And if they are brown skinned, we use bigger bombs. We leave unexploded bombs and mines in their forests, deserts and cities so their children will be killed or maimed, too.

This was the America of the 20th Century, and unless you change it, it will be the America of the 21st Century. The time for you to understand that we are not superior to anyone is almost gone, and you and your children and their children must start changing your ways before we squander our accidental and undeserved *foison.*

93. Beware of this Phrase…

"I Am Going to Be Honest with You" is an overused American expression that possibly means:

a. I have been lying to you up to now.
b. Let's get real.

But I rather keep on believing that the speaker of such words is a confused person who has little regard for the word he/she uses.

94. Women, Abortion is your Issue

I am against killing, and I am against abortion, but I also know that I used to ejaculate millions of sperms, and if one of them swam the best and met an egg, I had just participated in the making of another human being. I was the father. The lady who spread her legs, however, and knowingly or unknowingly allowed one of her eggs to intercept my Spermy, the swimming champ, had committed herself to a change in her life that she may or may not have wanted. She may not have been aware of the realities of nurturing this fertilization for nine months, raising it for 18 years, and then having it killed in the street where she lives or sent by the government to die in the hills or the valleys of another previously unheard-of country.

The land we live in is dominated by men, and the men say that aborting a fetus is murder. These mentally challenged assholes pay no heed to the killing they consented to by continuing undeclared wars, or by allowing the proliferation of guns, or by murdering murderers. These mostly male assholes have set up convenient morals, and any deviations require another law to banish the ways of those who wish otherwise. These assholes are the American Christians. Their religion began with a fellow turning over the money changers' tables. It was that act that got him crucified—if either actually happened. The present Christians, however, have no problem with charging usurious fees or even swindling their mothers out of their life savings with outright robberies or scams.

The Christians progressed to making the human body a work of God, and those who began to explore it, thus laying the foundations for our present medical practices, were punished. Yet today, the descendants of those believers have no issue with having their hearts stopped and a stent inserted so that they get an extension on living. They cannot have babies the normal way, so they accepted the glass tube and artificial insemination. I have always wondered how the Roman Catholic Church worked its way around the fact that daddy masturbated into a cup to get his non-swimming sperm to the egg.

It is up to women to solve this issue. Men are opportunists who will sell their mothers for a buck or violate all ethics when the price is right for a quick coitus or fellatio. Because of our natural desire to screw them and leave them, we men should have no power or involvement in legislating abortions.

It is up to the women to get elected to office, to refuse to send the results of eighteen or more years of nurturing and loving to die in some war or go to prison. The women are the mothers and, therefore, the righteous owners of the contents of their bellies. Male politicians should not have the right to stick their noses into that solely female event. To date, motherhood has done next to nothing to help obtain the power women need to stop men from dominating them. Look at how men influence women:

Men dish out religion.
Men run schools.
Men run governments.
Men start wars.
Men dictate life.

What have women done? They spread their legs to satisfy their men and have their child returned in a flag-draped casket eighteen years later, even though the women were never in power to vote on whether their children were to live or die. This is truly fucked up. So, tell the men to fuck off and go have your abortion if you wish. And to those women who will sooner or later chastise you, tell them to fuck off, too. Reason is on your side.

95. Looking for American Evil

When I give the finger to a driver who is being a moron, I rarely think it through. After I calm down, I usually think about the power that I had in the cocoon of my vehicle and usually feel ashamed of what I did. Because of those feelings, I only give the finger every 2,000 to 3,000 miles now, which is a great improvement. When I think of the underserved power that I give myself in the isolation of my vehicle, I try to connect it to the evil that exists in America when individuals go astray and murder for smaller infractions than those that cause me to stick out my middle finger.

So, what factors make me so different, mean or selfish? Perhaps the answer to that question is the way we live in America. In my little town in Italy, everyone knew everything about everyone. Even though we had fields that kept us out of earshot of each other, houses with one-foot-thick walls and no phones, facts and fictions traveled, and your secrets remained secrets only to you. When you think in your xenophobic ways that the Mafia in Italy is truly a covert organization, this is not true. The Mafiosi in a small town in Italy are fully known to everybody, and everybody is scared of reporting them. Self-preservation is still the number one human trait and will always be, regardless of what heroic tales are written about some of us. I am scared to give the finger to a neighbor when he screws up on the road, not because of ethics or respect, but because I am scared it will have consequences.

Perhaps we ought to be nosy and intercede in the lives of others. How stupid is this scenario: Johnny lives by himself and is an OK loner of a neighbor until he flips out one day and kills other people. Out of the blue, his grammar school teacher stands up for the TV cameras and says what a good boy he was in the second grade. Since then, Johnny bought or stole the guns, and no one noticed. When Johnny came home, he locked his doors, and his window shades were always pulled down. And no one noticed. So, the neighbors knew nothing about Johnny, and eventually Johnny got the courage inside his cocoon to pull the trigger and kill.

I know that what I just wrote is all bullshit to shrinks, but I also know that within all of us lives an evil version of Walter Mitty. Because our neighbors and relatives are too busy with their lives, once in a while Mitty takes over and manages to murder within the circle that was our little world. No one has any explanation for this.

96. Americans, Start Thinking

When the TSA searches us or the NSA spies on us, or when Congress screws us, we go right along with it with little or no open rebellion. Most of us don't realize that the government is screwing us all. You ought to think about your understanding and mute and consensual participation in the abuses that the government and your neighbors heap on you.

97. Cheer our True Heroes

Americans like to call our soldiers heroes. I think people who manufacture and deliver alcoholic beverages to the markets are the ultimate heroes. These people provide beer, wine and hard liquor so you can take it home and live in a stupor for a while. To me, these people are the ultimate heroes. They know they are doing good things, yet they ask for no recognition. See, there are real heroes in this world.

98. Am I Well Educated?

My opinion of my knowledge can best be explained by an analogy. Assume that grains of sand are bits of knowledge. I see myself on a deserted beach with a toy shovel full of sand. That is my assessment of my knowledge. Then, I imagine that there are people who have one grain of sand and people who have one or more pickup trucks full of grains of sand. Once in a while, there are truly exceptional cases in which someone has a semi truck loaded with grains of sand. When I really get heavy with my two-bit mental computer, I even figure out that knowledge, intelligence quotients, education and experiences are all rather stupid processes. Imagine yourself and nine other people lost in a forest. After days of starvation, the dumbest guy in the group comes up with an idea that saves the lives of all ten people. Whose mental abilities saved or will save your ass?

So, be less judgmental, for at the end your life, the only thing that is truly important to you will be in the hands of others, and what if they are dumber than you but manage to save your smart ass? What will you do with your knowledge then? Revise it?

99. American Stupidity Has to Be Looked at with Clear Vision.

How much do we spend to keep flying safe? How much do we spend to keep food safe? How much do we spend to keep cars safe? How much do we spend to keep electricity from zapping us? Why, then, is it not possible for us to stop the killing of tens of thousands Americans per year? Let me put it this way. I have lived in America for 56 years. If we assume a low estimate, that 10,000 Americans per year were killed with guns, then during my stay here 560,000 Americans have been killed.

Why don't Americans start a website called something like The Shamed Names? After each new killing, we could post the name of the gun owner and the names of the people the gun killed. Or memorize the names of the people in your community whose guns have killed other people and ostracize these gun owners and their kin.

They may misread a 225-year-old constitutional amendment, but you have the means to knock some sense into these selfish antisocial people.

100. No Atheists in Foxholes

Bullshit. When I was a child, I remember screaming for mom when I was hurt or in danger. As I grew up, and the priests and society put religion in me, I started imploring God when in danger. That adage about being a deist in a foxhole is bullshit; you do whatever you trained yourself to do at times like that. So many other quick-witted pearls of wisdom are, in reality, a bunch of bullshit we sell. Take the one about the early bird getting the worm. Bull. The early bird goes after the worm solo; if he was with a flock, he could not be an early bird. The early hawk sees a very simple case of his lone prey waiting to become his early breakfast. Of course, the hawk doesn't see the oncoming car in the early morning and gets smashed.

Life is never as simple as portrayed in adages that seem to be cure-alls. But life goes on, and some really believe the wisdom of adages. So, if you think airplane disasters occur in triads, when do you start counting? If the black cat crossed your path and you did not see it, would you still have bad luck? It is all crap, and you should not waste any time thinking about it if you can think.

101. True Conservatives

In case this has not convinced you that we, those who are about to die, have followed along the paths of our fathers and allowed basics human evils to survive, let me explain it more simply. If it were not for the ones who sought change from the ways of their fathers, you would still have rivers and lakes full of raw sewage and garbage. If we still obeyed the ways of our fathers, when your sister was raped, your family would keep it quiet, and women would not get anywhere close to the pay they get now. Conservatism is nothing more than idle reminiscing about an idyllic past that never was.

You have the option to take another path where the stupidity, ignorance, imbecility and depravity of the human race stops being an inheritance of morals. You can switch to the other path, which has been there all of the time. On this path, you are required to think and realize that you are not the only entity around. On this path, you are required to respect all, kill no one, stop the overpopulation of this earth, and, above all, understand that you are nothing more than a temporary guest in the hotel room.

You can start the remainder of this 21st Century C.E., by making it the century of the people, or of humanity, or even of good stewardship of the motel Earth. Or believe as you were taught to believe and die the idiot that you were born.

Changing America
with a
Peaceful Revolution

Since the beginning of time, there have been two or more classes of people, and regardless of the variations, it always been Us and Them. "Us" are the people who live from paycheck to paycheck, which is simply the least amount of money that our employers will pay. A thousand years ago, our ancestors lived on the scant leavings of the harvests that they produced for Them. Today, Them are governments, the rich, politicians on the take, religious cult leaders who literally rob the believers, gangs of people who are more righteous than we are and societies that mistreat some of their members. Them are the ones who, in one way or the other, control Us.

At times, the Us have rebelled, and when they won, new ways were enacted. In the end, however, nothing changed, or the changes were eventually reneged on by Them. In a sense, the Us have never really understood that Them need Us. They need Us to work for them, use their products, and spend whatever extra money we earn so that Them can skim a profit even from our so-called luxuries. In a sense, we are the assholes of humanity, but we are needed. A joke I heard years ago went like this: the organs of a human body had a rebellious moment, and each stated its critical contributions to the wellbeing of the entire body. This was done by each organ claiming that if it stopped functioning, this or that would happen. The anus kept quiet, and when everything had been said and no resolution found, it said, "I am the most important organ of the body because if I shut down, there will be a huge backup and you will all die."

The Us are treated as the anus of society. We are important only when it is necessary to do the fecal deeds of society, and for that we are treated as vulgar parasites on the moneyed people. What would you call working in a place and going home with a paycheck that is forty times less than the money made by the fellow who owns or runs the place where you work?

Or paying the same price for products while the actual weight of the contents are decreased by 10 to 50 percent, and you have to search for evidence of that robbery?

Or being incarcerated because you did not have the money to pay for competent lawyers?

Or having some of us executed by the legal system, which issues a posthumous apology years later?

Or being sent to wars that are waged for the sole purpose of insuring that Them stay rich?

Or having to pay exorbitant prices for medicines that we helped research, while the same medicine is sold at lower prices to foreigners?

Or a society that pays higher wages to trashmen than it does to the teachers of their children?

Or being tricked to vote for a politician by deceitful paid campaigns?

Or a society that fails to educate its poorest young and allows some of them to grow up to be thugs?

Or Them immorally suckering Us into paying a higher tax when the states we live in sell us the hope that we will win the lotto?

Or accepting the work of Enrico Fermi, an Italian alien in America who was working on atomic physics, while simultaneously imprisoning hundreds of Italian immigrants who had done no wrong but had been tagged as risks by the government. This was nothing in comparison to holding the 442nd Regimental Combat Team back from being the first to enter Rome, so that white American GIs would be the first. The 442nd happened to be the most decorated unit in the history of the Us Army and still is. This unit was composed of Japanese-American soldiers, but white officers commanded them. Here is how glorious America was in World War II. Twenty-five of these soldiers were detached from the unit in 1943 and sent to a camp where dogs were trained to sniff Japanese. The dumb American view of things was that one Japanese smells just like another, which is not much different from the sophisticated grandchildren of those dumb Americans, who today believe that every person with an Arabic name is a terrorist. God bless American ignorance. Many of the soldiers in the 442nd just happened to have parents, sisters and brothers imprisoned in detention camps while the soldiers fought for the principles of the country that imprisoned them.

There are hundreds of other ways to show you that Us, the anus of Them, are just a tool in a so-called free country. We will always be the underdogs of society because we are given just enough soma to survive the hardship of everyday living, and we are losers because when we fail to achieve the status of Them, we are told to try harder. Out of exasperation, some of Us turn to religion, which offers heaven, 22 virgins and other pleasantries, after we have done their deeds and are dead.

But there is a way out of this layered Us versus Them society.

America is the best capitalistic gathering of people in the entire world. Because of this, America accidentally created a true and palpable god. This god is known as the US dollar. The way we dispense the US dollar for services validates the make-believe world of heaven. In America, you are given a little bit of this god every couple of weeks, and we all worship this god with the same fervor. Those who have more dollars, however, are more godly and, thus, have absolute control over Us. This is nothing new. It is only fair that those who have more religion than you and me should get better housing and so forth. But think about the way Them get more godly because of Us.

We, the anus of society, have spending power. For the rich to stay rich, we have to spend our wages, so that the money of the rich grows. We have purchasing power. Our purchasing power, though smaller than that of the richest, is like what a fertile soil is to the growing of harvests. Our spending is the fertile soil but we rarely take advantage of this great power that we have. This is because corporations make us feel that we need their product regardless of the reality. How else did we get to the point where we have the most gyms, the most restaurants, the biggest grocery stores, stacks of cooking books and pantries full of food, and kitchen cabinets filled with cooking gadgets? Like sheep driven by dogs, we obeyed and became the fattest nation in the history of Earth. By being fat, we became more valuable to those who make drugs, dispense medical services and sell us pills. The morbidly fat people are fertile soil for Them to make more money than they would make if we were healthy.

Do you understand that Us make Them more money even by achieving such a squalid honor as being morbidly obese? Again, like sheep being commanded by a dog, we spend money, and Them sniff new ways to get us to spend even more money.

We can stop this abusive cycle in which we are nothing more than peons to the moneyed people of America, and it can be done in increments and without blood.

First, educate those who desire changes on the deeds of Gandhi, Martin Luther King Jr., Mandela, and other peaceful people who have changed the world for the better. As an aside, the Gandhi thing is as overblown as the aura given to most American leaders. There had been bloody efforts and tactful moves by millions of Indians to get rid of the British, but since history is painting that one picture of him, who am I to disagree? Second, make everyone aware that other governments have changed with little or no bloodshed. Remember the USSR? How about the way Poland told the communists to bug off? Then, I would explain that the common folks will always have the power to decide their future because they are the majority, and they can control how they obey and react to the norms of the society they live in.

In order to convey this message to the populace, I would create a website that would be the operating center for a loosely-knit organization similar to Alcoholic Anonymous. The Internet provides us a tool that will allow each person to have a say without having to go to their individual representatives. This website would have a listing of things that need to be changed. A voting and identification mechanism would give the participants the option to select the following:

    a.   Prioritizing the items to change, which would be done on a majority basis.

    b.   When, where and how to force the change. Again, people would select the options and the majority would win. Even though I believe that the majority is always wrong, it will take centuries to get humans to think independently, so for now, the majority has to do.

The process should operate on a legal basis and should cause no harm to anyone. This is not a traditional revolution or a war. It is simply allowing the common folks to exercise their powers in a government system that is unresponsive to the needs of the common people.

For example, one item on the list could be to get the federal government to establish a limit on political contributions. Money is not a constitutional tool that can be substituted for freedom of speech. Money is an acid that erodes freedoms, corrupts governments, and makes people kill. The Supreme Court was out of its senile mind when it construed that money can amplify one person's or corporation's freedom of speech. Or perhaps we will start the list with pressuring the NRA to change its mind, or the fast food restaurants to prepare healthier foods, or Israel to leave Palestine, or China to leave Tibet, or politicians be held accountable. Participants on the website would vote to take action and vote on a date to begin the action. On the day they select, preferably a Monday, the following actions could be taken by those interested in supporting the issue:

    a.   Drink only water and eat at home before going to work or school. Take a sandwich for lunch and drink water the entire day. Continue this for the designated period of time.

    b.   Drive at the lowest posted speed limit. On interstates, this is usually 45 mph. Interstates would have major traffic jams, people would be delayed and public response may be garnered. If those delayed bitch to their politicians or the law, you win. If the sufferers of the delay decide to side with you, you still win.

    c.   Obey all traffic laws, such as coming to a full stop. Slow down at a light in case it turns yellow, and take all other precautions that are part of the driving routine.

    d.   If you use public transportation, take your time finding a seat on the bus or entering and exiting the subways. Just slow the systems down.

    e.   If you are flying, take your time going through security and the boarding process. Fumble to find the paperwork required, and do not take all metal objects from your pockets. Play stupid. Ask questions. Obey each thing they tell you to do, but be slow about it. There is no law that makes you speed through those debasing checks.

f.   At work, ask a lot of questions about your assignments. Pester your supervisors and coworkers with questions about whether you are doing things correctly or whether there are any changes.

g.   Call in sick, or go home sick after a few hours, at the slightest sensing of body abnormalities.

h.   If you are dealing with customers, call the supervisors for any decision that you feel should be made by a supervisor.

i.   Take long and restful breaks.

j.   Visit the restroom more frequently than normal. Just slow down.

k.   At home, walk everywhere, which makes you buy less fuel and makes you healthier.

l.   Learn to live with wider ambient temperature ranges so that you use less energy.

m.   Eat simple foods without any preparation, such as pork and beans, canned vegetables, fruits, raw vegetables, or meats that can be eaten uncooked.

n.   Establish a period during which you will have no cigarettes, beer, or any other liquor, recreational drugs, sweets or anything else that is not required for a healthy week of living.

o. Call your local and federal representatives once per day and ask what they have done for you today.

p. If you have children, impress upon them that what you are doing is to better their lives.

q. Don't watch any TV.

r. Do not go to movies, paid sporting events or social gatherings where merchandise is sold or you need to buy food.

s. Have small groups of people gather in pedestrian areas so that they slow down traffic. The group must be of a number that makes it legal to gather without a permit. Do this in multiple places so that the police are overtaxed.

t. Go to libraries and get books or audio/visual media to occupy you. Don't buy any products that are not necessary to your living as Spartan a life as you can for a week.

u. If you cannot do all of these things, try to do at least one; when added to the efforts of others, the goal may still be accomplished.

Do this for a week at a time, and you will enjoy a week of less stressful living, and the world will change because the money does not move. When money stops moving, everyone will pay attention to your wants and needs. Try it and see what happens. Since each of these events would last for a work week, go back to your normal behavior the next Monday morning. Wait for a month or so, and if you didn't get satisfaction from the last event, repeat the process for a two-week period. You may lose some weight and a few habits that you may realize are nothing more than programmed behavior, and you will gain self-respect when you face up to those who treat you as a consumer instead of a human being.

With some refinements and good leadership, this would work. We, the masses, are like the worker ants in a colony of ants. We participate, produce and process the goods, and the colony works. The colony needs each ant to function on a predictable basis. The only thing you would be doing would be to decrease or totally stop the eagerness with which you do what you are expected to do and the way you use your time and money. We are so intertwined that we need each other. Our failure has been that we do behave exactly as desired by those who control us. Change and control your performance and spending habits and, in so doing, you will change your status from puppet to full-fledged participant, from peon to owner of your life.

This would work with as little as 10 percent of the population participating. Once it works, of course, the lazy or scared 90 percent will claim credit for it, as has always been the case. If you don't believe me, here is a bit of history for you. During the Vietnam War, American soldiers started fragging (killing) their officers. This type of thing had happened in other wars, but somehow it became a problem in Vietnam. After the war, the US Army went through a period of reinventing itself. This action gave the enlisted people more freedoms, authority and self-respect. Imagine, maybe 100 soldiers taking a murderous stand that they should never have taken, and they made the army change its ways.

Imagine you making Them change simply by not behaving, just for one week, as you have been trained to behave. Try it the peaceful way by decreasing the flow of money, and America will change. This is not guaranteed to happen in one generation, but if you persist and your children continue the struggle, change will come, and the America of the future will be better.

Try it.
It will not cause you intolerable suffering
and
you may begin to change our abusive ways.

www.ingramcontent.com/pod-product-compliance
Lightning Source LLC
Chambersburg PA
CBHW060624290526
45793CB00001B/129